RESTORE ME!

BUT PRIVATELY, PLEASE
(THE PEOPLE CANNOT KNOW)

DR. SUSAN AGBENOTO

WESTBOW
PRESS®
A DIVISION OF THOMAS NELSON
& ZONDERVAN

WestBow Press books may be ordered through booksellers or by contacting:

WestBow Press
A Division of Thomas Nelson & Zondervan
1663 Liberty Drive
Bloomington, IN 47403
www.westbowpress.com
844-714-3454

ISBN: 979-8-3850-1762-1 (sc)
ISBN: 979-8-3850-1763-8 (hc)
ISBN: 979-8-3850-1764-5 (e)

Library of Congress Control Number: 2024901505

Print information available on the last page.

WestBow Press rev. date: 5/10/2024

FOREWORD

Actors in the ancient Greek theater wore masks to indicate the roles they were playing. The most easily recognizable of these are the masks of tragedy and comedy—the Melpomene and the Thalia. In Restore Me! Privately Please, Dr. Susan Agbenoto brings another category of masks to our attention: the masks worn by Christian leaders in the ecclesial context. Unlike the Greek theater where everyone—actors and audience alike—were in on the deception for the sake of its entertainment value, the masks we encounter in the Church portray public faces that hide private problems.

Dr. Agbenoto's intention in writing this book is not to accuse, demean, or demoralize Christian leaders. Rather, with genuine compassion she reminds us of our humanity— wondrous and fragile as it is—and our need to stay close to the Lord. If we stay connected to God and are honest with Him and with ourselves, we can walk in wholeness and integrity before the ekklesia. Recently I shared with my Introduction to Pastoral Caregiving class some of the startling statistics associated with pastoral ministry in the American context: 80% of seminary graduates who enter ministry will leave the ministry within the first five years; 50% of pastors' marriages end in divorce; 70% of pastors continually battle depression; 70% of pastors have had an extra-marital affair since entering the ministry...and so on.

These statistics, and others like them, convince me that the book you hold in your hands is sorely needed in the Body of Christ today.

In an age that has become overwhelmed with marketing gimmicks, polished presentations, and "ten easy steps" to growth, success, and spirituality, I appreciate Dr. Agbenoto's sagely wisdom that calls us back to prayer, fasting, the Bible, and Christ-like humility. Don't let this book sit on your coffee table. Pick it up and read it. Apply its lessons and you will find your soul renewed by the power of the Holy Spirit.

Dr. Reggie Abraham
Pastoral Care and Chaplaincy
United Theological Seminary

RESTORE ME!
BUT PRIVATELY PLEASE!!.

Restore Me, But Privately Please! is a must read for everyone who has been broken. If you have been broken, and desire God to restore you back to wholeness, this is the book for you. Restore Me oh Lord, is the cry of all of us; though we do not desire it to be published worldwide.

In this book we encounter the Lord's tremendous love which leads us away from shame, and into restoration in the privacy of time spent in his presence. Dr. Agbenoto spoke from the heart in this book. Her supportive scriptures remind us throughout the reading that God is still good, and God is still willing to "Restore us."

Dr. Jacqueline Lynch
Pastor, Salem A.M.E. Church

CONTENTS

PREFACE

Have you come to the end of your rope? Are you tired on the inside, and going through the motions on the outside? There is always opportunity to pause and restart. Perhaps life has thrown you some curve balls and you cannot find your footing. There is always hope to rebuild. You have this book because I have prayed for you, and the Lord is opening His arms to you to bring your burden to Him.

The voice that says "give up" and "there is no use" is the voice of the biggest lie, owned by the greatest liar. There is always hope for tomorrow. If it were not so, you would not be promised this one fact: "Because he lives, you shall live also" (John 14:19).

As you move through these pages at your own pace, may you find rest for your soul. May you find peace on the inside. May you meet and be inspired by the King of Kings. May you be revived and inspired. May you bear even more fruit, accomplishing even greater works. Your best days are ahead. God bless you.

DEDICATION

I dedicate this work first and foremost to
my Lord and Savior Jesus Christ.

To Selase, Hezekiah and Josiah.

To my dad, Reginald Laryea and Aunt Shirley.

To my mum Alelia Quarcopome, whose support
during this journey I can only describe as legendary.

To my beloved grandmother, Emma, rest in peace.

To my United family and mentors, thank you.

Thank you to all who ever asked, "When will
you release the book?" Thank you for your
encouragement. You know who you are!

And finally, to all who find themselves
in need of encouragement, I dedicate
this work to you. You are loved.

1

WHO CARES FOR THE ONE WHO GIVES CARE?

Come to me, all who labor and are heavy laden, and I will give you rest. Take my yoke upon you, and learn from me, for I am gentle and lowly in heart, and you will find rest for your souls. For my yoke is easy, and my burden is light.

—Matthew 11:28–30 (ESV)

It is amazing how many times Minister Anyone will preach a powerful message, encourage a lost soul, make a sad one laugh, and afterward slump behind the steering wheel of a car and weep like a baby, oftentimes alone. Pastors, church leaders, and all who serve in some capacity serve selflessly but often with a declining emphasis on spiritual self-care. Very soon, the humanity aspect kicks in and spills over into rivers of depression, unforgiven grudges, feelings of betrayal, aloneness, sickness, and other unfortunate elements. The even more unfortunate aspect is the pedestal they are put on, which prevents them from sharing their burdens and forces them to fake strong fronts while crumbling on the inside, until it is almost too late. At this point, the devil is blamed for the fall, and shallow speeches of empathy and restoration are shoddily dosed to the broken minister. Everyone, of course, at this point is now a spiritual doctor.

But Jesus, our wonderful Savior, foretold of this phenomenon.

> Come to me, all who labor and are heavy laden, and I will give you rest. Take my yoke upon you, and learn from me, for I am gentle and lowly in heart, and you will find rest for your souls. For my yoke is easy, and my burden is light. (Matthew 11:28–30 ESV)

This passage, hidden in Matthew 11, could easily be the most misquoted in regard to context. It *is* true that if you have a burden and lay it at His feet, Jesus will lift the burden. This passage is, however, dealing with something a little different. It starts by saying, "Come to me, all who labor." This sets the stage for the specific audience and the specific side effect that comes with being part of this group. The audience addressed here is "those who labor." These are not limited to pastors and leaders only but all who serve or labor in the kingdom of God. The emphasis of this book is on the leaders and elders because the domino effect starts there.

In apostle Paul's letter to Timothy, Paul says, "Let the elders who rule well be considered worthy of double honor, especially those who labor in preaching and teaching" (1 Timothy 5:17). We will stay within this framework of laborers.

If you are not an elder yet you labor in His house, then the title is a matter of technicality. This book is still for you. Yet still, if are an elementary school teacher, if you serve in the military, if you are a CEO, a lot of these concepts will apply to you as well. You are reading these words because the Lord wants you to. He wants to heal your soul, and He wants to restore and refuel you for the next phase of your life.

Jesus said, "Come to me, all who labor and are heavy laden," implying that what He is about to say is only for laborers, to start with. He also implies that being a laborer comes with being heavy laden. It will be easy to form a theological argument against this and refer to many scriptures of joy and peace that the Lord gives. It will also be easy to lay this solely at the feet of the devil. Both have their place, but neither negates the words of Jesus. The casualties are falling at a rapid rate right under our noses, affecting both small and large congregations.

I once knew a minister who loved the Lord and pastored a beautiful church. Over time, he encountered some of the obstacles of spiritual leadership and became heavy laden. Today, he no longer pastors a church and is barely in touch with the body of Christ. I know another minister who was on fire for the Lord and had a thriving church, but he fell into troubles and became heavy laden. He had to step down from pastoring, and after a period of restoration, he came back into the ministry, but as a very disillusioned and cynical preacher. I know also of a much beloved minister who was overcome with being heavy laden and was found dead in his hotel room, apparently of a drug overdose. There is not enough room to mention the deaths, suicides, stress-induced diseases, resignations, firings, and falling into temptation, even if the reference point is as short as one year. Pastoral Care Inc. publishes statistics of surveys done among ministers (not just pastors) across various denominations. Here are some of the results of their most recent publication.

- One out of ten pastors will actually retire as a pastor (90 percent do not).
- 71 percent of churches have no plan for a pastor to receive a periodic sabbatical.
- Over 50 percent of ministers are unhealthy, overweight, and do not exercise.
- 34 percent of ministers wrestle with the temptation of pornography or visit pornographic sites (that is 1 in 3).
- 75 percent report spending four to five hours a week in needless meetings.
- 23 percent report being distant from their families.
- 50 percent state they spend one hour in prayer each day.[1]

Some of these—I say with trembling and not an ounce of judgment or self-exemption—are even dying and crossing into hell despite their labors.

Is it not the doing of the devil, one may ask? The devil definitely plays a role. In 1 Peter 5:8, we learn "Be sober-minded; be watchful. Your adversary the devil prowls around like a roaring lion, seeking someone to devour" (ESV). The devil is always walking about looking for someone to "devour." He will have a hand in any misfortune concerning anyone. The verse that follows encourages us to be aware and resist the devil's antics through faith and steadfastness:

---

[1] Pastoral Care Inc., "Statistics in the Ministry," Pastoral Care Inc., accessed November 19, 2023, www.pastoralcareinc.com/statistics.

"Resist him, firm in your faith, knowing that the same kinds of suffering are being experienced by your brotherhood throughout the world" (1 Peter 5:9 ESV). Afflictions will come our way, and the devil will try to take advantage of them to get to us.

The heavy laden state that Jesus refers to, however, is not necessarily the attack of the devil. It is the constant weariness, pressure, and "overburden" as the Amplified Bible puts it, or even clearer, "the working under a heavy yoke," as the Living Bible states.

One of the essential functions of the minister is to provide care. The dictionary defines *care* as providing watchful attention, carefully regarding a thing, and providing supervision.[2] One can add to that loving others and making time for them. Jesus goes a step further in Matthew 9:36: "When he saw the crowds, he had compassion for them, because they were harassed and helpless, like sheep without a shepherd."

This extends the meaning of *care* to having compassion for others while feeding and strengthening those who need help. It also includes gathering together in one place the flock of the Lord, instead of the natural scattering and divisions that take place. Sometimes it involves giving money and provisions to others who are in dire need. Then there are times when you experience death in the process or help carry grief when you are grieving yourself. Over time, this can be draining since the care of the flock can be taxing and challenging. The minister's soul starts to become heavy laden.

---

[2] The American Heritage® Dictionary of the English Language, 5th Edition. https://www.wordnik.com/words/care.

The direct effect of being heavy laden is that you have no rest, no peace, and no joy. There is a hollowness that develops deep inside of you, even though you show the world your smile and your strength. This is all centered in the soul. The soul, like your spirit and body, needs intentional care and regular refreshing.

A quotation from a spiritual wellness site forces one to look at and measure the outward effect of what is going on inside.

> Spiritual wellness means hope, positive outlook, acceptance of death (loss), forgiveness, self-acceptance, commitment, meaning, and purpose. It also includes clear values, a sense of worth, peace, worship, prayer, and meditation.[3]

Along the way, as a laborer, you encounter situations of others that leave a residue in your heart. There are times when life deals very personal harsh blows that don't make sense, such as divorce and the psychological and financial setbacks it leaves in its wake; blows concerning one's children; the death of a close friend or family member; financial setbacks, including homelessness; and even the collapse of one's church or business. The combination of these issues with the continuous care and labor of others, can test the boundaries of your strength and leave you questioning if there is even any real meaning to your life and if you are not simply a failure.

---

[3] Wellness Universe, "What is Spiritual Wellness?" Wellness Universe, accessed November 20, 2023, https://blog.thewellnessuniverse.com/top-2-spiritual-wellness-resources/.

As the statement reveals, there is a real place of spiritual wellness you can bounce back to with the help of Christ. This is a place of forgiving yourself and others and moving on; a place of acceptance of death and loss, even though the inner pain remains; a place of finding meaning and purpose with your new normal—whatever that looks like— as you reanchor your spirit, your soul, and your heart in Christ. It is a place of the restoration of your soul.

The following pages will take us on a journey of what comprises the soul: its composition, enemies, and afflictions. We also look at the ways we can prevail despite these drawbacks and walk as the overcomers we are destined to be. In the end, we need to drop off the dross and junk we accumulate over time and simply come back to Jesus so He gives us the rest within our souls that only He can give.

Here is a quick note on what to expect in the subsequent pages. Though the language is conversational, the content dives into a biblical look at the topic at hand, a theological examination in some areas, and then an interdisciplinary look to give us a more holistic idea of restoration within the soul. The underlying thread you will observe is the injection of scriptures. Each scripture is thoughtfully, prayerfully, and studiously inserted on the simple basis that the Word of God has the power to heal. The Word of God is inexhaustible. Within each scripture are layers upon layers of exegetic interpretation and application. This is rightfully so with the different types of literary devices utilized in the writing of the sacred scriptures.

This book could have easily become a lexicon of scriptures, but the ones provided are not for informational purposes. Rather, they are placed deliberately for you to pause, read in your own Bible, meditate on, and allow them to do their healing work in you. Believe the scriptures. Speak them aloud to your hearing. Believe in the power of the scriptures. Believe in the God who does not lie. After each chapter, there is a post-chapter meditation that challenges you to pick some key concepts and even scriptures to think on and pray with.

Finally, interspersed within the writing are prayers. Pause and pray along as you receive the power flowing from God through His Word to you.

MEDITATION AND PRAYER

I will meditate on your precepts, and fix my eyes on your ways.

—Psalm 4:4

Selah.

Pause and Meditate. What have you learned about yourself from what you have read so far? Have any of the issues listed affected you? Who cares for you? You have taken the right step already. There will be these Selah moments after each chapter for introspection and prayer.

Pray with me: Lord, teach me how to pause and meditate on what You are trying to show me. Heal me and strengthen me as I read this book. Reveal Yourself to me in a new way. Amen.

2

REST: WHAT IS THAT?

Come to me, all you that are weary and are carrying heavy burdens, and I will give you rest. Take my yoke upon you, and learn from me; for I am gentle and humble in heart, and you will find rest for your souls.

—Matthew 11:28–29 (ESV)

Did you take your time to read the verse and notice that the word *rest* appeared twice? Many times, we receive nuggets from the Word of God when we pay closer attention and accord it the seriousness it deserves. Attentiveness to the Word of God is not only needed when one is deep in sermon preparation, or working on a presentation, or building up an argument. These pauses are for our edification. I challenge you to pause and deeply reflect on each scripture you come across in this reading journey.

Rest. When was the last time you took time to rest? When was the last time you simply took time off to reflect, to be refreshed, and to be refueled?

On a different note, when was the last time you experienced the peace and beauty of His very Essence? When were you last brought to your knees, experiencing an acute awareness of your sheer dependency on Him? When was the last time you experienced conviction in your heart as you intentionally delved into the Word of God? Or even through a song? Think of these words: *sensitivity, intimacy, dependency* on God. Have you perhaps shifted, just a little bit, from this?

We must reverently differentiate between the care we give to ourselves as human beings and the service we do. The anointing, the call, and the work are all unrelenting and operate through the part of us that is spiritual. The body, on the other hand, does not develop any superpower with the added load that comes with the work one does. You have to be wise enough to recognize the body's distress signals and care for it. That is why the scriptures refer to us as vessels of clay (2 Timothy 2:20). All this power and anointing operates through a vessel of clay. You hear of leaders who have signs of obesity, stress-related hypertension, or even anxiety attacks, and never pause to take care of themselves because "I have to take care of this other thing that just came up." Not to be insensitive, but "that other thing" is stealing your very life from you if you do not pause to take care of that obesity problem and reorganize your life to mitigate the hypertensive triggers.

The two words used in Matthew 11:28–29 are surprisingly different in a nuanced way. In verse 28, the word rest is anapauo¯, with the Strong's dictionary translating it as "to cause or permit one to cease from any movement or labor in order to recover and collect his strength.[4] The implication is of taking a real rest from labor, as in a vacation day, a time-out, going away, sleeping in, being refreshed. It is the word used when Jesus was praying in the garden just before his capture and He came back the third time to see His disciples sleeping—again. His statement to them at this point was: "Sleep on now, and take your rest: behold, the hour is at hand, and the Son of man is betrayed into the hands of sinners" (Matthew 26:45 KJV). He reckoned the time to labor in prayer was over, what was going to happen was now sealed, so they might as well continue in their rest and be refreshed for what was coming.

This *anapauo¯* rest is also used by Jesus after the devastating beheading of John the Baptist and the pressure it put on Him and the disciples.

Jesus, the ever-caring Shepherd, said to His disciples,

> "Come away to a deserted place all by yourselves and rest a while." For many were coming and going, and they had no leisure even to eat. And they went away in the boat to a deserted place by themselves. (Mark 6:31–32)

Jesus was telling them to remove themselves from the immediate area and find a place of isolation where they could take a break and regroup since there was so much going on that they barely had time to eat. Can this describe you on some days where you keep going without stopping

---

[4] King James Version with Strong's Numbers – KJV Strong's, "Strong's G0373 - Anapauo¯"

so you don't even have time to eat? Jesus recognized this and redirected Himself and His disciples to a place of rest. This is really taking a break. One can think of it in this sense: if you don't take a break, you will eventually break.

In verse 29, the word *rest* is *anapausis*, and Strong uses *intermission*[5] as one of the translated words. *Intermission,* on its own, is hard to grasp and has different connotations within orthodoxy that differ from non-orthodox interpretations. Looking closely at its use within scripture, however, the meaning becomes a bit clearer. Scripture, you will find, is the best interpreter of scripture. *Anapausis* is used only five times in the entire Bible. The first time is in this verse, referring to the rest of the soul. Note that this is slightly different from the rest from physical labor. This points to a rest that is within. The second and third time *anapausis* is used is in the description of the passage of an evil spirit. After being cast out of a person, the spirit came back and looked for room in that same person again. Keep this story in mind as we dig deeper into strongholds of the soul in later chapters.

In Matthew 12:43–44, the Bible says,

> When the unclean spirit has gone out of a person, it wanders through waterless regions looking for a resting place, but it finds none. Then it says, "I will return to my house from which I came." When it comes, it finds it empty, swept, and put in order.

The Luke 11:24 version of the story says, "When the unclean spirit has gone out of a person, it wanders through

---

[5] KJV Strong's Dictionary. "Strong's G0372 - Anapausis"

waterless regions looking for a resting place, but not finding any, it says, 'I will return to my house from which I came.'

The evil spirit was looking for a place that was not dry to call home. He was looking for an "inner person" or a "soul" to occupy—one who had some commotion going on, some "water" of turbulence he could call home. The last two uses of *anapausis* are in the book of Revelation, where a microscopic look is voluminous enough to be deemed out of the scope of this book. Looking at the use of the word *rest* in these mentioned verses, we see that, unlike physical rest, this is an inward rest. One finds it when one surrenders the current yoke and takes the yoke that belongs to Jesus alone. This kind of rest takes a bit more than sleeping in or taking a vacation day. It's about taking deliberate steps to reconnect to the One who called you. It is coming back to your first love, as the book of Revelation calls it, restoring intimacy with God, sensitivity to His leading, and being in that place of walking with Him.

Learning of Christ brings us that rest found deep on the inside. A barrier is then built against roaming foreign spirits who want to lodge in our souls and leave us even more broken than before.

MEDITATION AND PRAYER

Be still, and know that I am God! I am exalted among the nations, I am exalted in the earth.

—Psalm 46:10

I am the vine, you are the branches. Those who abide in me and I in them bear much fruit, because apart from me you can do nothing.

—John 15:5

Selah.

Pause and Meditate. What have you learned about yourself concerning rest? What have you learned about yourself concerning your connection with God? You have made it this far. Continue to be brutally honest with yourself. Breakthrough is on its way.

Pray with me: Lord, teach me how to simply rest in You. Help me prioritize the demands in my life, with spending time with You being the highest priority. Amen.

3

A MICROSCOPIC LOOK
AT MY SOUL

Take my yoke upon you, and learn from me, for I
am gentle and lowly in heart, and you will find rest
for your souls.

—Matthew 11:29 (ESV)

We hear much about the spirit, and also about the
flesh, but little about the soul. Early philosophers
Plato and Rene Descartes were of the belief
that "body and soul together make up one substance,"[6]
otherwise known as *dualism*. Aristotle and Saint Thomas
Aquinas disagreed with that concept. St. Thomas Aquinas
eventually concluded that

> the human soul is incorruptible...once God
> creates a human soul, that soul exists forever.
> Given that the human body is corrupted at death,

---

[6] "Body and Soul," Thomistic Philosophy, accessed November 20, 2023,
https://aquinasonline.com/body-and-soul.

> the soul's incorruptibility entails that after death,
> it will continue to exist without the body.[7]

Plato believed that the body was united with the soul, but Aquinas in contrast believed that it was not the case since one lived on (the soul), after the other had died (the body). This debate about what the soul is and does has existed for hundreds of centuries. Kenneth Hagin, pastor and founder of the Rhema Bible Training College, echoing 1 Thessalonians 5:23, explained that "Man is a spirit, has a soul, and lives in a body."[8] Though it does not explain everything about the soul, this explanation has been accepted in many religious circles.

In the anchor verse of Matthew 11, Jesus promises rest for your soul—not your spirit, not your body, but your soul. This makes the need to know what the soul is important. When Jesus promises rest in our souls, what does that really mean and what is the effect? The trauma one goes through, for instance, is usually deep-seated in the soul. This demands that we take a deeper look at our souls and how our souls affect our entire lives.

The word *soul* in Hebrew is *Nephesh*. It is rather difficult to translate this into English language, though the meaning is built around the concept of breathing, specifically, "to be breathed upon, and to be refreshed."[9] This gives the image

---

[7] Robert Pasnau, "Thomas Aquinas," in *The Stanford Encyclopedia of Philosophy (Spring 2023 Edition)*, ed. Edward N. Zalta and Uri Nodelman, accessed November 20, 2023, https://plato.stanford.edu/archives/spr2023/entries/aquinas.

[8] Kenneth Hagin, *How You Can Be Led by the Spirit of God* (Tulsa, OK: Faith Library Publications, 2008), 3.

[9] KJV Strongs h314, Olive Tree Bible Enhanced Study

of the system of *inhaling* and *exhaling*. The first reference to the word *soul* is found in the creation story of humankind.

> And the LORD God formed man of the dust of the ground, and breathed into his nostrils the breath of life; and man became a living soul. (Genesis 2:7 KJV)

This system of breathing is sustained after God created humankind by the act of breathing. God first created the body using dust. This was not the soul, just the body. Afterward, He breathed into the dust. Breathing involves the inhaling of air from the outside, into the body, and then exhaling the carbon dioxide from the body back into the air. God breathed not oxygen, or any form of air, but "life" into the body of dust, and it became alive, a "living soul," because that was what was breathed into it. The soul then acts as a "mediator between the internal (spirit) and external (body) worlds." It is the crux of life and death because the day breathing stops, life ends.[10] The medical process of intubation is to artificially generate breathing when the human body cannot effectively do so because of illness. This is done because the end of breathing, naturally or artificially, marks the end of life.

Some Bible versions use "me" instead of the word soul to convey the message that the soul is actually the person.

> I said, LORD, be merciful unto me: heal my soul; for I have sinned against thee. (Psalms 41:4 KJV)

---

[10] Dr. Reggie Abraham. Presentation on Care of a Soul.

> As for me, I said, "O LORD, be gracious to me; heal me, for I have sinned against you." (Psalms 41:4 NRSV)

The King James and New King James, for instance say "heal my soul," whereas the NRSV and other similar versions simply translate it as "heal *me*." These differences are neither necessarily wrong nor right translations but relate to the closeness in the relationship between a person's soul and his or her very life.

There are other important aspects of the soul that are referenced in the Hebrew translation to English. Going back to the concept of inhaling and exhaling connects *nephesh* to the throat. Since food is also taken through the mouth into the body via the throat, this makes the soul a seat of appetite within us. That implies that we may be able to train the soul to control our appetites for certain activities and behaviors. Another word used is *desires*. Appetites and desires are two of the key concepts that have led to microscopic studies of the soul.

Witness Lee, a Chinese Christian preacher of the early 1900s, spoke of the concept of the soul consisting of three parts: the mind, the will, and the emotions.[11] He cites Proverbs 2:10, which says "and knowledge will be pleasant to your soul," and other similar scriptures dealing with the soul and knowledge. Since obtaining and maintaining knowledge takes place in the mind, the connection of the soul to knowledge also connects it to the mind. Concerning the part of the soul which deals with our will, Lee cites Job 7:15 (NASB) which states "my soul would choose,"

---

[11] Witness Lee. The Soul having three parts. http://www.ministrysamples. org/excerpts/THE-SOUL-HAVING-THREE-PARTS.HTML

and Job 6:7 (NASB), which states "my soul refuses." Lee explains these as functions of the will. Another verse he notes concerning the will is 1 Chronicles 22:19 (NIV), which says "Now devote your heart and soul to seeking the LORD your God." Seeking or loving God is a matter of choice, and subsequently a matter of our will. If our soul is broken, it is hard to flow in that constant place of seeking Him. Lee finally addresses the connection of the soul to our emotions by referencing scriptures such as "tell me, you are my soul loves" (Song of Songs 1:7 ESV), "who are hated by David's soul" (2 Samuel 5:8 ESV), and "my soul rejoices in my God" (Isaiah 61:10 NIV). He uses these and many scriptures that capture the soul loving, filled with joy or hate, filled with desire, grief, misery, and so on, proving that emotions are linked with the soul.[12]

Putting these complex fragments together, the soul then is the intellectual, thinking, feeling, and decision-making part of you.

The soul also has the power to determine your eternal destination, according to the words of Jesus.

> Do not fear those who kill the body but cannot kill the soul; rather fear him who can destroy both soul and body in hell. (Matthew 10:28)

For this reason, the apostle Paul prayed,

> May the God of peace himself sanctify you entirely; and may your spirit and soul and body

---

[12] Witness Lee. The Soul having three parts. http://www.ministrysamples. org/excerpts/THE-SOUL-HAVING-THREE-PARTS.HTML

be kept sound and blameless at the coming of
our Lord Jesus Christ. (1 Thessalonians 5:23)

With this background, we can piece together the beginnings of a revelatory collage of the soul. It embodies the breathing mechanism of the human being, mediating between the internal (earth) and external (spirit) worlds, while being the base of the mind, the will, and emotions.

In that light, let's look at some aspects of our souls that we need to be aware of.

- Your soul is one of the components of your being that loves God, as we saw in the prior section. A heavy-laden soul will struggle with this.

    > He (Jesus) said to him, "You shall love the Lord your God with all your heart, and with all your soul, and with all your mind." (Matthew 22:37)

- You can lose your soul. Because your soul is a mediator between the earthly and physical realms, it is possible to lose your soul.

    > For what will it profit a man if he gains the whole world, and loses his own soul? (Matthew 8:36 NKJV)

- Your soul as well as you spirit will go to heaven or hell.

  > For you will not abandon my soul to Hades, or let your Holy One experience corruption. (Acts 2:27)

- Worldly and fleshly desires constantly war against your soul. We see that the soul is a seat for our appetites and desires, and therefore a battleground to fight temptations.

  > Beloved, I urge you as aliens and exiles to abstain from the desires of the flesh that wage war against the soul. (1 Peter 2:11)

- Your soul can become defiled. Because the soul comprises the mind, there is a symbiotic relationship between the soul and the mind. If the mind becomes defiled, this affects the soul.

  > To the pure all things are pure, but to the corrupt and unbelieving nothing is pure. Their very minds and consciences are corrupted. (Titus 1:15)

- Your soul, which houses your conscience, can be seared.

  > Through the hypocrisy of liars whose consciences are seared with a hot iron. (1 Timothy 4:2)

✐ ✐ ✐ ✐

Coming back to the principal verse "and you will find rest for your souls," Jesus says we should come to Him and He will give us rest. It is a reminder that even though we start *with* Him, as we labor, we *can*, and more often than not will, move away from Him. It seems that the farther away we are, the more heavy-laden we become. He says simply, "Come," and we will get rest from the heaviness. In the next verse, though, He changes the tone. It is no longer "Come," but an instruction: "take my yoke" and "learn of me." It's also no longer *I* will "give you rest" but "*you* will find rest for your souls."

The heavy burden results from heavy yokes we pick up along the way as we labor. We do not always recognize that this is happening. We may even forget some of the things that happen along the way, but the soul absorbs all of it and brings it up at the most inopportune times. As we come to Him and learn from Him by going back to spending time in His Word and prayer, a gentle washing takes place. This refreshes us on the inside, giving our souls rest. We should be mindful that the soul is the core of who we are, the breath of our existence, and the reflection of our earthly fruitfulness and outputs. Rest for our souls then means peace in our minds and emotions, a refreshing within us, a refueling and motivation to get up once again and move into higher realms of destiny and fruitfulness.

To have a greater picture of a yoke, and how it looks on our souls, imagine the wooden or sometimes metal structure placed over the heads of two animals, for instance two donkeys, to give double pulling power. This is common in farming communities. The yoke keeps the animals in place together so that where one went, the other did, as directed by the driver. It also increased the pulling power of the plow or whatever equipment the animals were pulling. We find ourselves similarly yoked in life. The yokes, however, are in our souls. We become yoked with someone we partner with in marriage, we become yoked with someone we have sexual intercourse with, and we also become yoked with someone we are laboring with or even for.

The most important yoke we need to acquire is the one belonging to the Lord Jesus. That means we are moving in the same direction as He is, and we are moving in great power because He is the one actually doing the work.

At some point in our labors, however, we gradually move the necks of our souls away from Christ's yoke and exchange it for a human-made one. It immediately becomes heavy around our necks, leaving us heavy-laden and without rest.

Earlier in the chapter, we looked at different aspects of our souls that we needed to be aware of. One of them is that the soul is a component of our being through which we actively love God. When Jesus was asked what the greatest commandment was, His answer was that, "You shall love the Lord your God with all your heart, and with all your soul, and with all your mind" (Matthew 22:37). In keeping with His consistent references to the Old Testament, Jesus's answer is found in Deuteronomy 6:5. Since we love the Lord with our souls and with our hearts, they are the natural targets of heaviness, making it difficult to love God wholly. When the work of the ministry has become a heavy human-made yoke, efforts shift to pleasing people rather than loving God. Things like politics and favoritism in church structures start to weigh in, and you question why you serve the Lord in the first place. The lines between loving the Lord and serving the Lord become blurred.

In this place of soul unrest, one becomes weaker in fighting the temptations the world offers. This is similar to when one's immune system is weak and the body finds it more difficult to fight diseases. A weak soul finds it difficult to fight temptations and becomes the right turbulent ground for some wandering spirit to make a resting place. These spirits may suggest we should just end it all since there is no hope, or even suggest coping mechanisms that are far out of the purviews of morality. These adverse coping mechanisms will be discussed in detail in subsequent chapters because of their injurious impact on one's soul.

King David once reached that point of weariness and lack of joy. At that point, he came before the Lord and prayed "Restore to me the joy of your salvation!" (Psalm 51:12). For us today, it could be preaching, pastoring, teaching in a religious or non-religious institution, or leading a religious or secular institution and doing so without the joy found within. You are just going through the motions, with one tired and discouraging day blurring into another. You, for instance, share your salvation testimony as a quota that must be met rather than out of joy. You drag yourself to church on a Sunday as if you are carrying a truck on your head, ready for battle rather than out of excitement and hunger for the Lord. David knew he needed to go back to that place of joy in the Lord, where he had rest within his soul, to minister effectively again to others and turn transgressors away from sin and unto God.

Rest in our souls provides the strength we need to keep fighting the good fight of faith. Rest in our souls is found in the Lord Jesus. There is no scar the Lord cannot heal, and no sin He cannot forgive. If you can recognize the Jesus-free burden you are carrying (which He has not asked you to), if you can recognize that you are experiencing brokenness, He is saying to you right now, "Come to me." David did just that. One practical way is to go down on your knees and confront that mountain in your life, even if your mountain is the Lord Himself, because at times, the anger we feel is against God.

Come before Him and confess it: "Lord, I have felt anger toward you for letting my sister die. Forgive me. Heal me." After speaking with the Lord, go back to His Word. You may even write it out in the form of a letter to the Lord. That pure Word does wonders in restoring our souls.

> Therefore put away all filthiness and rampant wickedness and receive with meekness the implanted word, which is able to save your souls. (James 1:21 ESV)

Go back to Jesus, the Word. His Word is still saving our very souls. There is restoration in His Word. There is healing in His Word. He said take His yoke and give Him your grief. Hand Him your pain, and take up His yoke. He said to take His yoke and drop the human-made, people-pleasing yoke you have adopted, and He will bring rest once again to your soul. Others are waiting for you to lead them to the light, but until you make that exchange, you will be ineffective in your assignment.

MEDITATION AND PRAYER

Moreover, the Lord your God will circumcise your heart and the heart of your descendants, so that you will love the Lord your God with all your heart and with all your soul, in order that you may live.

—Deuteronomy 30:6

Selah.

Pause and Meditate. Do you recognize brokenness within? Is there an opportunity for confession of hurt, anger, betrayal, or even hatred? The tough work begins here, but you are not alone on this road to healing.

Pray with me: Lord, I confess to _____. I need Your help in forgiving and letting go. Heal my brokenness. Circumcise my heart, that I may love You with all my heart and all my soul. Draw me closer to You. Amen.

4

SPIRIT OR SOUL?

Therefore rid yourselves of all sordidness and rank growth of wickedness, and welcome with meekness the implanted word that has the power to save your souls.

—James 1:21

The Difference

The spirit is connected to the heart. Romans 10:9–10 explains that when we confess with our *mouths* the Lord Jesus and believe in our *hearts* that God raised Him from the dead, we are saved. This is the conversion experience from unbeliever to believer. Within the heart and spirit, the salvation process takes place.

The soul, on the other hand, is the remaining part of our non-physical being that undergoes a continued salvation process better known as *sanctification*. Whereas the spirit is connected to the heart, the soul is connected to the mind, which embodies our thoughts; to our wills, which includes our desires; and to our emotions, which are the manifestation of our feelings. Sometimes the words *spirit* and *soul* are used in certain phrases. When read in different translations, the words *heart* and even *life* are used instead, which deepens the complexity between the two. Much as the spirit and soul are close, their functions are separate and some verses point that out.

> Indeed, the word of God is living and active, sharper than any two-edged sword, piercing until it divides soul from spirit, joints from marrow; it is able to judge the thoughts and intentions of the heart. (Hebrews 4:12)

The above verse shows that the spirit and soul are so commingled, similar to the way our bones and marrow are, that it takes the piercing sword of the Word of God to be able to differentiate between them. There are times when what we are dealing with originates in the spirit realm, and there are times when we have to deal with it on a soulish level. The discerning of the two, as well as the resolution of the issue, is rooted in the divine power of God. Are you dealing with grief deep within your soul, or are you dealing with a spiritual root of depression manifesting as mourning, for instance? The Sword of the Spirit, which is the Word of God, can discern and bring healing to the source of the issue.

Ongoing Maintenance of the Soul

As mentioned earlier, beyond the salvation experience, there is ongoing maintenance that needs to take place within the soul, as the opening scripture suggests.

> Therefore rid yourselves of all sordidness and rank growth of wickedness, and welcome with meekness the implanted word that has the power to save your souls. (James 1:21)

The King James Version uses "filthiness" instead of "sordidness," describing the dirt and grime that the soul accumulates over time, necessitating regular cleansing. This filthiness is a result of the connection of the soul to the mind, which is constantly bombarded, willingly and unwillingly, with images, sounds, ideas, and messages, both clean and unclean. How many times have you watched a movie or even just regular TV or YouTube and an ad popped up with explicit images you would have preferred not to see? You did not actively search for it, but because your mind chances upon it, it leaves an imprint. You now have to do the work of cleansing your mind and soul. We are encouraged in 1 John 1:9 to come before the Lord and ask him to cleanse us. He is "faithful and just to forgive us our sins and cleanse us from all unrighteousness." This cleansing is the first step in preparing ourselves so we can receive the words of God, which then continue the work of sanctification in our lives. Ask the Lord to cleanse you and ask Him to let His word do its sanctifying work in your life.

Apart from the rank growth that takes place within our souls, our souls can also undergo trauma. Examples include encountering a tragic event, such as being in the presence of one who is dying, witnessing casualties of a fire or an auto accident, and having to minister to them or surviving families. It could be horrendous events witnessed during one's formative years or being the victim of such. With trauma, it's not so much a cleansing process that is needed, but healing, so that the sanctification process can be without hindrance.

> I said, LORD, be merciful unto me: heal my soul.
> (Psalms 41:4a KJV)

In Psalm 41, the psalmist acknowledges the trauma his soul goes through as he enumerates the betrayal and ill-wishes even to the point of people awaiting his death. The assault happens when we are accused wrongly, when we experience abusive leadership, when we go through a divorce, when we are broken-hearted, and when we watch something we built disintegrate before us. When one undergoes this kind of assault against the mind or even emotions, it can leave a traumatic trail of brokenness that must be repaired. It also causes us to build guards around ourselves to prevent a repeat of the traumatic event. David knew that if the Lord did not heal him, it would affect his entire being. He then cried out to God to heal him. The transliteration of the word *heal* includes concepts such as mending, repairing, curing, and making whole.[13]

---

13 NRSV Strongs. #7495

As you open up yourself to the healing power of God, may He mend you where you are broken, repair the brokenness on the inside, cure you, and make you whole, in Jesus's name.

Hope: The Pivoting Mechanism of the Soul

When Jesus asks us to bring our burdens to Him, he is offering us hope. When our souls are laden because of either sordidness or fatigue, there is hope for restoration. When our souls undergo trauma, there is hope for healing. Finding hope in Christ for tomorrow can be the ultimate difference between girding yourself to take one more step or giving up.

> May the God of hope fill you with all joy and peace in believing, so that you may abound in hope by the power of the Holy Spirit. (Romans 15:13)

This verse is an infusion straight into your soul to bounce back by the power of the Holy Spirit. The Lord infuses us with the power of hope, which converts our inner turmoil into a joy and peace that does not make sense. The Lord steps in, binds our hidden wounds, and nurtures them as a nurse would do in a clinic. Only this is done in the realm that is not seen. We do not see Him pick up forceps and Band-Aids, but we experience peace and joy in the aftermath. The scriptures say, "Now hope that is seen is not hope. For who hopes for what is seen? But if we hope for what we do not see, we wait for it with patience" (Romans 8:24–25).

You may still be asking, "How?" and struggling to keep hope alive. The Lord knows the weaknesses within us when we are already at the bottom of the hope barrel. He has made provision for us in the very next verse: "Likewise the Spirit helps us in our weakness; for we do not know how to pray as we ought, but that very Spirit intercedes with sighs too deep for words." The Holy Spirit has been given to us in our weakness to keep hope alive. He is there in our weakness when we should be praying and we do not have the strength or direction to. He is right there, to stir up hope and to keep the image of light at the end of the tunnel before us. In the words of Jesse Duplantis, "Times of crises require strength. And there is no greater strength than faith in the light at the end of the tunnel."[14] The Holy Spirit helps us on this journey.

Jesus, through his Word, has the power to turn around your situation and to transform your life. He will take all the broken pieces and build you up again. All cannot be lost when we have a God who is into building and repairing.

> And now I commend you to God and to the message of his grace, a message that is able to build you up and to give you the inheritance among all who are sanctified. (Acts 20:32)

The Lord will comfort you, build you up, restore you, and even give you an inheritance. He has called you to bear fruit, and when He is done with the restoration process, you will bear even more fruit to the glory of His name.

---

[14] Jesse Duplantis. I never learned to doubt. Destrehan, LA: Jesse Duplantis, 2022. 39

No circumstance is beyond the Lord's reach. You can be restored. You can be made whole. There is hope for tomorrow—a better tomorrow. Jesus is waiting for you to come to Him, so take that first step. Jesus is the master and caretaker of our souls and already promised us that if we come, He will take away what should not be there (the heavy-laden state), and grant us rest.

MEDITATION AND PRAYER

Therefore rid yourselves of all sordidness and rank growth of wickedness, and welcome with meekness the implanted word that has the power to save your souls.

—James 1:21

Selah

Pause and Meditate. What have you learned so far? Is there cleansing or healing that needs to take place in your life? Perhaps an opportunity for surrender?

Pray with me: Lord, where I never gave myself truly to You, I come to You freely in surrender. Rid me of the dirt and dross. Heal me where I am broken. Make me a new person within and without, in Jesus's name. Amen.

5

ENEMIES OF OUR SOULS

Consider and answer me, O Lᴏʀᴅ my God! Give
light to my eyes, or I will sleep the sleep of death,
and my enemy will say, "I have prevailed;" my foes
will rejoice because I am shaken.

—Psalm 13:3–4

Between the poetic prayers of the Psalms and the
life story of King David, we receive insight into the
dealings of the soul. This is especially for those
who walk in leadership roles. In the book of 1 Samuel 24,
David finds himself hiding from his arch-enemy King Saul.
He is given the opportunity to kill Saul when Saul comes
into the very cave David had access to for some privacy.
This gave David a perfect opportunity to rid himself of his
enemy once and for all, but he chose not to. This is the
same King Saul who had attempted to murder David and
was pursuing David until he had to live his life in hiding.

Like David, you may find yourself in a place where the
very people you serve are after your life. They criticize your

attempts to help, they plan your termination, and they treat your help with disdain. In the title psalm for this chapter, the psalmist cries, "Give light to my eyes, lest I sleep the sleep of death." Here the sleep of death can refer to the total emptiness you may experience at the lowest point of your career, ministry, or even life in general. You find you have nothing to give because the dryness and the nothingness on the inside feels like an eternal sleep. You find you are not as fruitful as you were. You wallow in shallow depths while spouting out intelligent words without power. The psalmist cries out that the Lord should enlighten his eyes. He cries for light and life. He further explains that God should move, lest his enemies gloat, saying they have prevailed against him, or even rejoicing because of all the suffering.

In addition to physical enemies, there are enemies of our souls who pursue and plunder us and attempt to prevail over us, as we see with David. The light that the psalmist is crying for is the light of revelation in order to identify the enemy, expose him, and expunge this enemy so he may walk in liberation, life, and fruitfulness once again.

David laments, like most of us have done in our hearts, in Psalms 141 and 142 over this situation. There are some themes we will draw out that seem to be common pain factors we face. We can call these "enemies of our souls."

Being Overwhelmed (Faint-Spirited)

> When my spirit is faint (overwhelmed) you know
> my way. (Psalm 142:3a)

There are times when you may experience many things at once: a personal crisis, a family issue, a financial setback, or a legal case all coupled with ministry assignments and congregants needing attention because of what they are also going through. Sometimes it can be one issue—the death of a loved one, for example—that causes you to be overwhelmed. David was overwhelmed by the fact that he was being pursued for no logical reason and his very life was at risk. That state of being overwhelmed is processed in your soul and puts you in danger of making impulsive decisions to bring relief to your burdened state. David could have decided to kill Saul, bringing an end to the ultimate trial of his life. What he did instead was recognize that he was overwhelmed. He took a step back to think through his actions, and then brought the issue to the Lord in prayer.

Being overwhelmed, or faint-spirited, is a real thing. Acknowledge it and assess what your working solutions are. In some cases, you may need to see a counselor or spiritual adviser. You may need to take a week or two off to regroup. You may need to say no to an assignment because you are not at full capacity to handle it. In the case of the loss of a loved one, you become immediately aware that the "normal" you knew is gone because of the nature of the finality of death. Your soul processes the assault of that just as it does when there is divorce or an unexpected unfavorable medical diagnosis. As long as you have life, all is not lost. As long as you look to the Lord, who gave Himself unto our greatest enemy, death, there is hope for tomorrow. It will not be the same "normal" that you knew, but it will be a modified "normal" through which He takes you by the hand and leads you through the current day, and the next, and the next one after. Acknowledge your new season and, like David, bring your heartfelt pain to the Lord. Cry out to Him, and allow Him to heal and strengthen you.

Loss of Way

> When my spirit is faint (overwhelmed) you know my way. (Psalm 142:3a)

It's challenging to picture the strong and self-assured King David feeling he has lost his way. It happens to the strongest and the best. You may have started off with zeal and excitement to help others, to build something, to make the world a better place. The challenges of that, interspersed with out-of-nowhere roadblocks, political maneuvers to achieve a small goal, and persecution from the very people you are trying to help, can make you feel lost. You may have started with clear goals and strong convictions, and entered into a season of weariness of soul where you wonder why you are even doing what you are doing.

There was a season in the disciples' lives right after Jesus had been crucified where they felt lost. They were filled with a deep hopelessness and wondered if the whole visitation of Christ was even worth anything. It took Christ revealing Himself to them again in resurrected form for their spirits to be stirred up and for them to find the path they were so sure about in the not-so-distant past. There is value in the visitation of Christ to the disciples. We also need those encounters with the Lord periodically to revive a certain kind of hope and zeal. At times, we may need to pull a hard brake and spend some time resting in Christ, making room for that encounter, allowing him to stir up our spirits, and establish clear guidance in our hearts.

Hidden Traps Being Overwhelmed (Faint Spirit)

> In the path where I walk they have hidden a trap for me. (Psalm 142:3b)

David wrote this psalm when he was in a cave. King Saul, whom he had served faithfully for many years, sought to kill him. He was caught up in physical traps, political traps, and all kinds of intrigue. You may find yourself feeling trapped due to your circumstances, as if you cannot make any meaningful steps forward or in any direction. There are many traps set up along the Christian journey because of the enemies who fight us.

One such trap is unguarded relations with the opposite sex. It could start with simply being welcoming, checking in periodically, and even praying with them. In unguarded moments, these actions could develop into a need to talk to or a need to be with this person. There may be nothing sexual intended, though those trap doors are also open. The "need," however, to speak with or be with the person slowly fuses into an emotional relationship, termed an emotional affair. Then there are the sexual affairs. There are traps to let you fall, lead you away from your calling, or dull your passion and zeal for the Lord. There are traps that consist of drug and alcohol temptations, traps to cut corners, or traps to desensitize you to the Word of God and fellowship with other believers. Some of the traps spring up suddenly, leaving you wondering how you got there. Other traps are slow-working, gradually crippling you until you are not sure where or when you started to fall into this pit.

There is no person, and no leader, who is too strong to fall. Traps are successful in alienating you from hearing truths that you need to hear for your salvation, from hearing wisdom that would take you forward, and from meeting critical individuals who would springboard you into the destiny set before you. Whatever trap you have fallen prey to, and whatever pit you find yourself in, Psalm 103:5 tells us of God, who "redeems your life from the Pit." May the Lord reach out and deliver you from wherever you are. May his hand of deliverance cause you to come out and experience restoration, healing, and refreshment in Jesus's name.

Loneliness

> Look on my right hand and see—there is no one
> who takes notice of me; no refuge remains to me;
> no one cares for me. (Psalm 142:4)

Even though David was surrounded by the men he led, he was still alone. Many leaders deal with the enemy of loneliness. This happens over time and can become a chronic issue if not corrected. One cause is the inherent need to separate personal issues from "business." Who does the pastor tell when he or she is having issues with his or her spouse and is considering divorce? Who does the deacon talk to when a fellow deacon is bullying him or her? Who does a leader report to when he or she is dealing with racism, gender discrimination, wayward children, and a whole gamut of issues that others look up to him or her to help solve? There is also the aspect of the person's issue being broadcasted because the person he or she spoke to could not contain such information in his or her vessel. Adding to that is the issue of a perceived lessening of respect when someone learns about the leader's problems.

A typical example is Joab, the commander of David's army and the son of David's older sister Zeruiah. Joab knew many of David's issues and treated him with less respect and even with hostility toward the end of his life. Once, he challenged David to go to battle with him or else he would claim the victory as his own (2 Samuel 12:26–28). Another time, he killed David's son Absalom when David had expressly stated that Absalom should not be touched. He later returned to rebuke David for crying so shamefully over the death of his son (2 Samuel 19:1–8). Leaders need restoration, but the need for privacy often plays a role in whether steps are taken or not because of the Joabs around them.

You can be surrounded by many, like David, but be alone. You can be married and yet be alone when there is a disconnect between you and your spouse. You can find yourself with plans and ideas that no one buys into, which can render you alone mentally. Loneliness, however, is an enemy. It is a heavy weight upon the soul, and it partners with depression. Some people end up on antidepressants as a solution. Some of these may genuinely be necessary, whereas for others, the true cure is social interaction. One of the first observations God made after creating Adam was that "it is not good for man to be alone." The Lord also says, "God makes a home for the lonely" (Psalm 68:6a NASB).

The Lord is very aware of the power of loneliness and gave us a cure from the start.

First, let the Lord know that you feel alone. He is the one most concerned about it. Intentionally develop a relationship with Him. Second, ask the Lord to bring a person into your life who you can talk to about your challenges without judgment. Moses had Jethro, who saw his struggles and even counseled him to delegate some of his work. King Hezekiah had the prophet Isaiah. King Uzziah had Zechariah. The Lord knows how to give you a person, or even as the NASB puts it, a "home," where you can freely share your challenges and issues without fear of rejection, judgment, or the issue being revealed elsewhere. Be sensitive to whom God will send your way, but also be intentional in making the Lord your primary confidante. There are times when that person is a therapist in that season of your life. Whoever it is, acknowledge God's hand in depleting loneliness, which lets you operate in a mentally tortured space.

Being Brought Very Low

> Give heed to my cry for I am brought very low.
> (Psalm 142:6a)

Another enemy of the soul is reaching a point so low, you are not even sure if there is hope for tomorrow. These are times when all the trials culminate in a focal span of time. Perhaps this involves having to care for a loved one while going through financial difficulty, or being accused falsely of wrongdoing while having relationship challenges.

It could be a deal or a project you have invested so much in that ended up failing, leaving you to decide to either continue or give closure to the path you have been on. Through it all, you may feel like you do not have anything more to give, and feel that you are disconnected from your support system. A combination of any two or more of these can bring you to such a low that you lose sight of the God who created you with a special purpose. The "light" burden Jesus talks about seems far away and you are weighed down by your burdens.

First of all, take your eyes off the weights, because your meditation on the issues is weighing you down more than the issues themselves. There is nothing more you can do to physically change the issue, but do not compound it with mental agitation. Hebrews 12:1–2 has some insights for us.

> Therefore, since we are surrounded by so great a cloud of witnesses, let us also lay aside every weight and the sin that clings so closely, and let us run with perseverance the race that is set before us, looking to Jesus the pioneer and perfecter of our faith, who for the sake of the joy that was set before him endured the cross, disregarding its shame, and has taken his seat at the right hand of the throne of God.

There are some learning points in these two verses. First, take your eyes off of the issue and mentally set aside the weight. Second, acknowledge that you are still in the race, even though you feel at your lowest, and cry out to God for the grace to hold on in strength and patience. Third, fix your eyes on Jesus now that they are off the issue.

Know that Jesus is the author of all that concerns you, and will also help you finish what He has begun in you. Lastly, be encouraged that for every trial you endure, there is glory waiting at the end of the tunnel. There is no season that does not end. We experience rain for a season, then it ends and is followed by either sunshine or cold. No season lasts forever. Your season of suffering is for a span of time, and at the end of it lies glory. Believe it. Believe in the power of Christ to help you through it. Believe in the promise of Christ to see you through it.

Encountering Strong Enemies

> Save me from my persecutors, for they are too strong for me. (Psalm 142:6b)

King David was being persecuted by an authority greater than himself. It is one thing to be harassed and fought against by those of equal or lower ranking. However, when the opposition is coming from a higher rank, the effect and the impact is more destructive. It's destructive because we usually look to those of higher authority and ranking to be our protectors and defenders. When they turn out to be the opposite, it translates into betrayal, causing distrust, disillusionment, and in some severe cases fear and trauma. David had to cry out to God when Saul was after him, "Save me from my persecutors, for they are too strong for me." He aptly cried out because Saul was coming after him with the power and backing of the entire army of Israel.

In some instances, the issue you are dealing with has a root source in a curse, another strong enemy. The scriptures teach that when there is no cause for a curse, it will not come to pass (Proverbs 26:2). This does not necessarily mean that it rolls off one's back, but rather that an intentional counteraction through prayer, denouncement, and the like can eradicate the presence of a causeless curse. If there is a cause, it is not as simple, and the divine backing of heaven is needed to bring one from under the power of such a strong enemy. Curses can be a manifestation of ancestral covenants from decades before one's existence. In some instances of slavery, family members sold their own to the buyers, and their lives have never been the same because of the heartfelt curses released through hurt and betrayal.

Some of the curses are through innocent bloodshed. Decades later, you can find yourself walking in the aftereffects of some of the activities of the generation that lived before you. David said in another place, "He delivered me from my strong enemy, and from those who hated me; for they were too mighty for me" (Psalm 18:17). It takes the power of God to bring you out of some of these obstructions that simply do not make sense. Like David, cry out to the God who is able. Bring your case before Him. Let the patterns be broken. Let the darkness stop in your generation without moving on to your children and their seed.

Personal Prison

> Bring my soul out of prison, so that I may give thanks to Your name. (Psalm 142:7a NASB)

The NASB captures the imagery well when it says, "Bring my soul out of prison." Our souls can be bound in captivity caused by our formative years, our biases, our upbringings, traps we walk into, different levels of stagnation, and even walls we have built up around ourselves as a result of distrust. The prison season is when we experience a lockdown of movement or fruit-bearing. It can manifest as depression, an inward dryness and dullness, and a lack of motivation. You see what is ahead of you to be done, but have neither the energy nor the desire to do it. Imagine being put in a jail cell, seeing through the bars, but being unable to move beyond the defined space of your cell. The soul can experience such imprisonment, where you can't pray, read, or muster the energy to do even the most basic of things. Give this also to the Lord. He will bring you out.

I pray that the Lord Jesus will bring you out of every such prison you find yourself in, in Jesus's name.

MEDITATION AND PRAYER

Return, O LORD, rescue my soul; save me because of your lovingkindness.

—Psalm 6:4 (NASB)

Selah

Pause and Meditate. Which of the enemies of the soul have you been combatting? Perhaps it's time to set your eyes upon Jesus to walk you through this phase.

Pray with me: Lord, I admit there is a war on the inside of me, as my soul combats many enemies. Deliver me, Lord, from these invisible enemies and strengthen me to run this race set before me. In Jesus's name. Amen.

6

THE ROOTS AND PLANTINGS WITHIN OUR SOULS

My soul makes its boast in the LORD; let the humble hear and be glad.

—Psalm 34:2

In the previous chapter, we looked at some enemies of our souls. King David experienced a variety of soul afflictions, though he also had his high moments. When he eventually says, "My soul shall make its boast in the Lord" (Psalm 34:2), it is from having gone through deep darkness and coming out victorious by the power of God alone. This is your portion as well. David had gone through some pretty rough times, including pretending to be a madman so he could obtain refuge away from his persecutor, King Saul. He went through all that and experienced true victory and restoration of his soul.

For us, it is an aspiration to be able to go through many issues, experience diverse afflictions, and find ourselves still standing, declaring, "My soul makes her boast in the Lord."

When we do a quick soul check, where do we stand? Are we celebrating and boasting? Did we experience a total knockout in the last round of issues?

There are occasions when the total knockout causes us to develop negative characteristics. This chapter and the next will look at some of these characteristics as part of the diagnosis preceding healing and restoration. These negative characteristics progress into vices and inappropriate coping mechanisms, corrupting us until we experience a disconnection from the Lord and even our callings. The progression takes place on different levels and in different stages. Hebrews 12:15–16 gives us some insight.

> Looking diligently lest any man fail of the grace of God; lest any root of bitterness springing up trouble you, and thereby many be defiled. Lest there be any fornicator, or profane person, as Esau, who for one morsel of meat sold his birthright. (Hebrews 12:15–16 KJV)

This talks about "the root of bitterness," which ends up "springing up" into further trouble, implying a progression. The soul can be likened to a patch of soil in which different kinds of seeds are sown. The seeds arise from interactions with people, events, and situations, and can either nestle deep in the soil of your soul or be washed away with the rain of the Word and other godly interactions. This passage explains that when we are not careful with what we accept within the soil of our minds and hearts, the seed nestled will germinate into a root. This further grows into deeper issues that trouble us, letting us fall short of the fullness of life while depriving us of the grace reserved for us from God.

Some of the seeds that can germinate into roots and afflict us as a result of the weariness in our souls include bitterness, resentment, unforgiveness, lust, and hurts. Being a laborer in the Lord's vineyard does not exempt you from being exposed to these seeds. Being a leader or teacher does not exempt you either. In some instances, you may rid yourself of one type of seed only to be confronted with another. Bitterness grows very slowly, and so does resentment. When you serve in a place, bitterness can be birthed when you feel you are not treated fairly, if you feel there is favoritism or even nepotism, if you feel you are not adequately compensated or rewarded, and so on. A lack of appreciation from both the people you serve and those who placed you in that position can also slowly boil up resentment.

Another seed that can quickly take root is lust. Lust wars for the place of purity within our souls. The statistics of ministers who either view pornography, have had extramarital affairs, or have engaged in sexually profane interchanges are staggering.

Let's look at a publication released by PIR Ministries. The findings are based on a study of 1,050 pastors in Pasadena, California conducted by Dr. R.J. Krejcir of the Francis A. Schaeffer Institute of Church Leadership Development.

- 30 percent had either had an ongoing affair or a one-time sexual encounter with a member
- Only 26 percent said they had personal devotions and were fed spiritually
- 70 percent said the only time they spend time studying the Word is during sermon preparation

Krejcir also references Focus on the Family studies, which revealed that 35 percent of pastors personally deal with sexual sin. Krejcir states that "Pastors who tend to be very educated seem to have the ability to embark on sin on Saturday and preach the Word on Sunday without thinking anything is wrong."[15]

It is now becoming more difficult to prop up the holiness demanded by the Word as a standard because, unfortunately, the opposite is currently the world's standard. To not engage in sex-related activities is now unique. Being a virgin, and abstaining from sex with a non-marital partner, is now almost archaic. But these roots are *troubling us,* as we see in the scripture, and truly causing us to live in a subpar version of the grace that we could have been walking in.

The world may be changing, but the standard of the Word does not. Lust is a reflection of corruption, or *defilement,* of the soul. Hebrews 12:15-16 continues this thought: "See to it that... no one is sexually immoral or unholy like Esau, who sold his birthright for a single meal." The sexually immoral and the "unholy" are categorized together and called "profane" in the King James Version. Esau's unholiness was because he sold his birthright for a piece of bread. Sexual immorality is equated with that level of unholiness, the level of despising our spiritual birthrights.

Some will argue and say that God's grace is over us irrespective of what we do. I do not doubt that. We would not even exist without His grace. However, there are

---

[15] Dr. Richard J Krejcir. PIR Ministries. Statistics on Pastors. https://pirministries.org/wp-content/uploads/2016/01/FASICLD-Statistics-on-Pastors.pdf

different levels of grace, and we determine which level of grace we walk in by our obedience to His Word. In Acts 4:33 for instance, it speaks of "great grace" being upon the apostles. Great grace implies there are levels of the dosage of grace that accomplish different things in one's life. This level of great grace upon the apostles translated into power demonstrations. This grace is different from the "saved through grace" level of grace that brings us salvation. Seeds of sexual immorality have to be crushed and expunged from our lives, and Christ grants us the power to do so.

Apart from sexual sins, unforgiveness is another seed that can take root within our souls and trouble us. There are many opportunities for unforgiveness to take root in our hearts. Relationships are the breeding ground for offenses, and offenses are the breeding grounds for unforgiveness. You can probably think of one or more persons you need to forgive for a situation, a betrayal, or an incident. These may be people you expected to know better, to do better, and to stand by you, but who did not. You may be in a Joseph-like situation where your family members left you for dead, and their manner of showing you mercy was to come back and sell you as a slave. Perhaps your spouse left you for a trusted friend or your children turned their backs on you. Why is forgiveness important? Why is it important to rid oneself of bitterness, or lust, or any of these roots?

As we think about these questions, we need to understand the urgency to expunge these toxic roots from the soil of our souls so they do not progress from *seeds* into what the scripture refers to as fruits of "defilement." At the progressed stage of defilement, we are not dealing with mere roots any longer but roots that have now generated plants. These are much more difficult to remove. They start to change us. When a soul has reached this defiled stage, the Hebrew transliteration is that it is like being dyed to another color. The color of your soul, in effect, changes. It darkens. The word also means "contaminated." Glimpses of the change start to bleed through into your personality, your thought process, and your actions. The NET Bible version of this verse adds that "no one be like a bitter root springing up and causing trouble, and through him many become defiled." Not only does the person affected become stained, but they also in turn stain others who interact with him or her.

The springing up of this defilement plant in our souls, if not pruned, progresses further into a *vine* or tree. At this point, it has become a stronghold in our souls. What started as mere seeds sown in the soil of the soul now has the power to control one's thoughts, actions, and decisions. When it was in the seed stage, it could be uprooted with relative ease to prevent roots. In the vine stage, however, the tentacles wrap around the subject and spread far. A routine weeding is insufficient; 2 Corinthians 10 says it must be "destroyed."

> For the weapons of our warfare are not merely human, but they have divine power to destroy strongholds. We destroy arguments. (2 Corinthians 10:4)

Derek Prince, in his teaching on the Resurrection, mentioned that when a thing is corrupted, such as a fruit, the process cannot be reversed.[16] At that point, a new one is needed. A complete restoration of the soul is needed. The next chapter will delve deeper into strongholds.

Going back to the question of why we need to forgive and let go, the elemental answer is that the alternative is too costly. These progressive stages illustrate why it is important to deal with the seeds of negativity early. When our souls start to be weighed down, we need to seek help early. The complex tentacles of these seeds tend to spread out with time and become more difficult to deal with. The impact affects our lives, our spiritual walk, our relationships, and our destinies. To forgive someone ultimately means to set yourself free to walk in the fullness of all that God has for you.

Where there has been severe corruption within our souls, there is hope for renewal and restoration. Like the psalmist, there is opportunity to cry out, "O Lord, restore my soul!" (Psalm 23:3).

---

[16] Derek Prince, "Resurrection!" posted April 12, 2013, YouTube video, 50:48, https://www.youtube.com/watch?v=DiyDrwwiU6E.

MEDITATION AND PRAYER

So if the Son makes you free, you will be free indeed.

—John 8:36

Selah

Pause and Meditate. When you do a quick soul check, where do you stand? Are you celebrating? Did you experience a total knockout in the last round of issues? Which of the stages—seed, root, defilement, vine (stronghold)—do you find yourself in? The Lord Jesus waits for you to take that step toward Him, to set you free.

Pray with me: Lord, I need You to help me see where I have been hung up. I desire to be set free from the spreading disease which defiles my soul and spirit. I give You my heart and I let go of negativity. Set me free and lead me in Your way. In Jesus's Name. Amen.

7

STRONGHOLDS AND
SNARES OF OUR SOULS

he previous chapter mentions occasions when the total knockout of our souls causes us to develop negative characteristics. These negative characteristics then progress into vices and inappropriate coping mechanisms, corrupting us, until we experience a disconnection from the Lord and even our callings. It is a continuation of this that leads us to track the growth progression of this to the level of strongholds. This tracking is necessary because the knowledge, and diagnosis, lends direct insight into the healing and cure.

Prior chapters have covertly covered biblical, theological, and practical studies of the soul. When we shift into the healing within our souls, this pattern of looking at it from a biblical, theological, and practical view will be maintained. In this chapter, as we look at how strongholds form, we will divert into an interdisciplinary look to observe how the chemical composition of the human body and emotions intersect with the dealings of our souls.

Recalling the descriptive image of a stronghold, we are reminded that it is like a grapevine that has grown all over its structures of support so it is difficult to see where it begins and ends. Imagine your soul being overtaken and wrapped around by such a vine. Many of our souls are in such states. Another image of a stronghold is a large, impenetrable castle or fortress surrounded by a moat that cannot be breached from the inside or the outside. If the soul, as we learned earlier, is the mediator between the internal (earthly) and external (spiritual) worlds, a stronghold then becomes a block to its mediation ability. With the soul as the seat of appetites and desires, you can begin to see the picture of what a stronghold does. It dilutes the power of restraint, blurring the soul's signals of "stop" and "go."

Here, negative behaviors and even addictions begin to manifest. The lack of connection to Christ, who is our ultimate strength, causes one to develop coping mechanisms that feed on these appetites and desires. Perhaps there was a time when prayer was your go-to activity when you found yourself in a bind. Now you find addictive activities to fill that void. It could be as harmless as watching TV, watching an episode from your favorite series, reading novels, playing video games, or surfing social media. These become more convenient to reach out to than prayer. More disturbing is the craving to do these without the power to do something else.

The American Psychological Association (APA) describes addiction as "substance dependence." The term is sometimes applied to behavioral disorders, such as sexual addictions, Internet addictions, and gambling addictions.[17] The desire alone to cease from the addiction is not enough, and some sort of intervention is required. Sometimes the intervention is clinical, at times it is spiritual, and on many occasions, a combination of both. A personal desire to overcome strongholds is necessary to begin the process

---

[17] https://dictionary.apa.org/addiction

of disengagement, though it is only the starting point. This is because at the addiction level, one's desire is tainted by the very stronghold that has overtaken it. There has been an alteration of the soul's appetites and tolerance levels. The well-intended "last" alcoholic drink becomes the first of ten more. Just as the well-intended "last" pornographic look becomes the last look for that day only. There's a continuous urge for "just one more."

A Clinical Look

Studying this from a clinical point of view, scientists have identified a chemical in the brain associated with addiction and pleasure. It's called dopamine. In her book *Dopamine Nation: Finding a Balance in the Age of Indulgence*, Dr. Anna Lembke explains that "the more dopamine in the brain's reward pathway, the more addictive the experience."[18] There are things that we do repeatedly because they bring us pleasure. The more illicit the pleasure, the higher the inflammation of the dopamine centers of the brain, increasing the appetite and motivation to recreate this pleasure,[19] on an even higher level. It starts, for instance, with a drink, then a drink becomes two to recreate the buzz, and then it eventually ends up being the entire bottle. The need to recreate the feeling of pleasure is what births the addiction or repeated behavior. Usually, what was done

[18] Anna Lembke, *Dopamine Nation: Finding Balance in the Age of Indulgence* (New York: Penguin Publishing Group, 2021), 2.
[19] Kent C. Berridge and Morten L. Kringelbach, "Pleasure systems in the brain," *Neuron* 86, no. 3 (2015): page.646

the first few times does not quite create the same effect because the body has recalibrated its threshold levels. The second phase involves doing it more, or using a stronger dose, because there has been a reset in the brain, redefining the level of tolerance needed to achieve this pleasure. With drugs, for instance, this progression leads to overdoses in some cases because the increased doses collapse the lungs and lead to death.

This dopamine effect is not just limited to drugs. Our addictions could be to food, sugar, our cell phones, inappropriate sexual behaviors, gambling, emotional affairs, reading and watching inappropriate material, and others. The "drug" of choice can be as harmless as watching TV, as noted earlier. When the activity becomes a consistent activity to numb yourself to the issues you are facing, and you cannot stop when you want, you have to face the fact that you are dealing with an addiction. The balance between recreational use and dependency must always be examined because even a harmless activity can turn into an addiction. The cell phone has created a normalized addiction for most. Through it, many other behaviors have been cultivated with access to all sorts of vices through its readily available internet.

Psychology teaches us there are a few unfortunate consequences resulting from indulging in experiences that bring us illicit pleasure. The "high" created is followed by a "low" or a "crash" that leaves one craving to return to the behavior. Have you put your phone down after surfing the internet for hours, only to pick it back up after ten minutes? Lembke explains that "we crave our drug just to feel normal—a level balance."[20]

A new normal has been created within us. This is because, according to Tabitha M. Powledge,

> drugs can cause a host of changes to parts of the brain that control body functions, especially the brain stem and spinal cord. These alterations produce physical dependence on the drug.[21]

Our brains are actually altered by these behavioral patterns. The second consequence of some of these indulgences is the guilt that they create on the inside. We experience guilt because we all have standards by which we live. When that standard is breached more times than we can control, we are unwilling to deal with the fact that there is an issue. We present a "normal" front to others as we struggle internally, gradually sliding into a double life. We begin to wonder who we really are. When that question is not resolved quickly by seeking help, the end can be fatal. The third consequence is that the addiction reaches a point when the vehicle or drug does not even bring the expected pleasure, and we start to feel empty, depressed, and sometimes suicidal. We start to realize that it is increasingly difficult to receive pleasure from everyday activities.

The fourth unfortunate consequence, and perhaps the most grave, is that these substances do not merely alter the brain on a temporary basis. They alter it permanently as the

---

[20] Lembke, 57.

[21] Tabitha M. Powledge, Addiction and the brain: The dopamine pathway is helping researchers find their way through the addiction maze, *BioScience*, Volume 49, Issue 7, July 1999, Pages 513–519

brain records the patterns of craving followed by pleasure rewards and associates triggers with these rewards. This means that, after many years and even decades of abstaining from an addictive substance or behavioral pattern, a combination of a craving, a trigger, and the sight of the substance (or something associated with it) can lead one right back into it.[22]

Mike: A Case Study

I once knew a person I will call Mike. I met Mike when sharing the gospel on the streets on a sunny day. He was drunk. Through a few challenging processes, Mike enrolled in a rehab institution. I would visit Mike from time to time and we were both proud of his progress. After nine months, Mike was released and graduated to a halfway home so he could work while living in a controlled environment. I still visited Mike even though I would see him in church most Sundays. Then in the eighteenth month of freedom, Mike's mother, with whom he was close, died. This activated overwhelming emotional pain that in turn triggered the craving for the very thing he had abstained from for eighteen months. He succumbed to it, and this time, was unable to bounce back. He ended up worse, was kicked out of the home, ended up on the streets, and vehemently refused to think of anything close to rehab.

This is an unfortunate but not isolated event that causes me grief. Mike is, however, a case study of the permanent

---

[22] Robinson, Terry E., and Bryan Kolb. "Structural plasticity associated with exposure to drugs of abuse." *Neuropharmacology* 47 (2004): 33-46.

alteration of the brain caused by most addictive behaviors and substances. Circling back to the term *defilement*, the transliteration, we learned, is akin to being dyed to another color. A dye alters the natural color of a thing. Whether we are talking about the effect on the soul or the chemical impact on the brain, we see the same result. Even when the behavior is harmful, the addicted soul repeatedly engages in it, despite its effects. The apostle Paul, recognizing the snare of addiction, said, "all things are lawful for me, but I will not be brought under the power of any" (1 Corinthians 6:12 KJV).

The apostle recognized that one could develop a dependency on anything, good or bad. He also referred to the pull of dependency as a "power." When you think of the strong desire you have for a substance, person, or thing that in some cases can cause harm, without having the willpower to draw away, the word *power* in the verse definitely makes sense. Apostle Paul's goal was that, when he started to see the signs, he would uproot the seeds quickly enough so he would not be brought under this power. What do you engage in that has become a substitute for leaning on Christ? What power are you contending with within your soul?

Because the soul functions as the seat of our appetites, the corrupted, enhanced appetites need to be dried out, the inflated dopamine centers stabilized, and a complete restoration initiated. Still bearing Jesus's words about finding rest in our souls in mind, we are looking at this in detail to receive liberation and rest. When the soul is in the stronghold state, it is ensnared. It is imprisoned. It is held hostage—held hostage by a demonic entity that one has to fight to be released from the pit or snare.

> Behold, for peace I had great bitterness: but
> thou hast in love to my soul delivered it from the
> pit of corruption: for thou hast cast all my sins
> behind thy back. (Isaiah 38:17 KJV)

The prophet Isaiah describes how he had the seed of bitterness, just as we saw in the Hebrews 12 passage. However, he acknowledges that his soul, which housed this seed of bitterness, had been ensnared in a pit. The Lord in love, through divine intervention, comes down and delivers us from that pit.

> Our soul has escaped as a bird from the snare
> of the fowlers; The snare is broken, and we have
> escaped. (Psalm 124:7 NKJV)

Psalm 124:7 gives us an even clearer picture of the ensnared soul and the entity that holds it in the stronghold, called the "fowler" here. A soul ensnared by alcohol is in a snare or pit guarded by a demonic entity or "fowler" of alcoholism. A soul ensnared by lust is in a prison guarded by a demonic entity of lust.

Recall the description of the evil spirit that was roaming about looking for a "water-turbulent" soul to reside in? The scriptures show us that when the evil spirit came back the second time, it came with seven spirits even stronger than him to occupy the territory (Matthew 12:43–45). The case study on Mike epitomizes this. When the spirit of alcoholism came back, it came back with reinforcements and the recovery was far more challenging than before. This speaks to the permanent chemical alteration of the brain the addiction caused. The brain recognized the trigger that brought him back to the place of addiction, leaving him even worse off. This also speaks to the difference between this kind of soul addiction and a seed of bitterness that can be uprooted fairly easily. In the case of strongholds, the strongman guarding the fortress must first be bound, the snare must be broken, and the soul extracted.

The good news is that though it may not be easy, all things are possible with God. The psalmist rejoiced and declared, "The snare is broken, and we have escaped." He followed it up in the next verse, saying, "Our help is in the name of the LORD, who made heaven and earth" (Psalm 124:8 NKJV). There is help available right now.

Breakthrough

There are two immediate steps you can take. If you are dealing with substance addiction (alcohol, drugs, pills), take the step of going online to find a clinical rehab center near you and contact them. Make the call. If you are dealing with depression, search online for a therapist and make that call. This call is your confession of a struggle and the beginning of freedom from chains you can live without again.

The second step is a drastic action step that will be the focus of the next chapter. It is time to take the action of repentance, fasting, and prayer. You can ask a trusted spiritual elder to walk this road with you. Strong chains need strong measures. The most important thing is to focus on the saving power of our Lord Jesus Christ and believe that He can and will set you free.

MEDITATION AND PRAYER

Then I called on the name of the LORD: "O LORD, I
pray, deliver my soul!"

—Psalm 116:4 (ESV)

Selah.

Pause and Meditate. This was a heavy chapter to work
through. It either is either the case for you or it's not—or
you can see the road signs ahead. Open your heart to
revelation and liberation.

Preparation: Prepare your heart to participate in a time of
fasting and prayer for at least one day. If you sense you
need more than one day, definitely follow that prompting
as well.

8

LIBERATION THROUGH THE POWER OF REPENTANCE

Whoever conceals his transgressions will not prosper, but he who confesses and forsakes them will obtain mercy.

—Proverbs 28:13 (ESV)

iberation is not only possible, it is available to you, and you have begun the journey. Liberation precedes restoration because it allows the old to seep out and the new growth to begin. There is a liberating power in repentance. Repentance is the turning away from a thing. The important aspect of repentance is that it starts in the mind and heart. Repentance is a change of mind and thinking concerning a thing. Before a person can benefit from a rehab facility, for instance, there has to be a mental acceptance of negative behavior and a mental decision to make a change. Granted, the change does not happen overnight, but without the mental decision, the rehab will be short-lived.

Repentance likewise, starts with the mind and translates into behavior. In the book *Truth Therapy: Renewing Your Mind with the Word of God*, Dr. Pete Bellini talks about "stinking thinking." He explains different types of thinking and how they affect our behavior. Sometimes, the negative behavior is indulging in self-pity, constant negative projection, and so on. A change in thinking can affect behavior and decisions a lot. [23] You have begun well with picking up this book and getting this far. Now there are steps to take to continue in the same strength.

Repentance here involves identifying the soul's negative behaviors, deciding to turn around, and asking the Lord Jesus for His mercy and help. The liberation comes because confession brings a release. The scripture says whoever covers a thing will not prosper (Proverbs 28:13). As long as it remains unconfessed, your soul does not prosper. However, the moment light is shined on it, with a decision to turn around, the healing process begins.

At times, our repentance is simply for lack of thankfulness. This can be because we feel that we have suffered too much and don't have anything to be thankful for. Your very breath is a testament to the fact that it is not over until the Lord says it's over. You have to choose between projecting your current circumstance into the future and the acceptance and profession of the truth of God's Word. His Word says, "In everything give thanks" (1 Thessalonians 5:18 NKJV). Your position should change from exalting your circumstance as truth to exalting the Word of God as truth. Take your eyes off the storms and turn them to the Lord

---

[23] Dr. Pete Bellini. "Truth Therapy: Renewing Your Mind with the Word of God." Wipf and Stock Publishers, 2014. 47

Jesus. Make a deliberate decision to give Him thanks. It is His will for you.

> In everything give thanks; for this is the will of God in Christ Jesus for you. (1 Thessalonians 5:18 NKJV)

Apart from repenting from a lack of thankfulness, there are other things that fall into our need for repentance. For instance, repenting for allowing other activities to be our coping mechanisms instead of turning our eyes to the Lord. Repenting for leaning on certain people because of the compassion they showed us until our relationship with them became inappropriate. Repenting for substance use that has placed us in a compromising place of addiction. With an open heart, the Holy Spirit leads us in what we need to repent for. Don't hold back or make excuses—just flow with Him.

Let us pray a prayer of repentance

Lord, I confess that I have been in a place where issues and circumstances have caused me to exalt them over You. You alone, Lord Jesus, should be exalted in my life. Through the pain, grief, guilt, my lack of gratitude, numbness, and even addiction to things, I ask for Your help and Your forgiveness. I confess that You alone are my Lord and Savior. Give me the grace to turn my eyes on You, and to keep my eyes on You, so I will be saved from the things that seem to want to consume me. I thank You for cleansing me and giving me yet another chance. To You be the glory. In Jesus's name. Amen.

MEDITATION AND PRAYER

I will be glad and rejoice in Your mercy, for You have considered my trouble; You have known my soul in adversities.

—Psalm 31:7 (NKJV)

Selah.

Pause and Meditate. Identify areas where you can begin your journey of repentance. Bring them to the Lord. Prepare yourself to fast as you read the next chapter.

Write: This is an opportunity to get a notebook or journal and start your journey of diagnosis through recovery. After prayer and meditation, write down the things that were brought to your attention, and write down steps you are taking to bring change. A journal can be a great therapist if you are honest with yourself.

9

LIBERATION THROUGH THE POWER OF FASTING

And when He had come into the house, His disciples asked Him privately, "Why could we not cast it out?" So He said to them, "This kind can come out by nothing but prayer and fasting."
—Mark 9:28–29 (NKJV)

This verse, also found in Matthew 17:20–21, is a unique story of a boy with an ailment that Jesus's disciples could not cure. This was reported to Jesus, who responded by saying that this type of ailment took prayer and fasting coupled with faith. There is some scholarly debate over this verse that I will quickly mention since some Bible versions omit it with a footnote. Some scholars believe the verse was added by the scribes to emphasize the practices of the early church in fasting and prayer.[24] Other scholars believe it was part of the original

---

[24] NET Full Bible Commentary on Matthew 17:20

manuscript. Considering this is present both in Matthew 17 and Mark 9, it takes more to argue that the transcribers added the same word in two different instances. The debate itself draws attention to the enemy's desire to reduce the importance of fasting to something that *zealots* do.

The Dake Study Bible Notes, which identifies thirty-five different Bible fasts, defines fasting: "To fast means to abstain from food."[25] It goes on to note, "All believers are supposed to fast, but no regulations or set rules are given as to how long or how often. That is determined by individual desire and needs." Supporting scriptural references include Matthew 9:14–15, 1 Corinthians 7:5, and Acts 13:1–5.[26] Fasting works in conjunction with your faith and with prayer.

Three things are accomplished during a fast. Fasting humbles our souls before God. Separating ourselves from food for a period of time (skipping breakfast, skipping breakfast and lunch, and so on) requires some discipline and brings our bodies under subjection to God (Psalm 35:13).

Fasting suppresses our appetites and desires so we can dedicate that time to prayer and seeking God, as we saw Jesus do in the wilderness (Matthew 4:1–11). One result we saw from Jesus's fast was the power to resist the devil and his temptations. The other result was the power to go into the towns to minister. Fasting releases spiritual power in your life.

---

[25] Fasting and Prayer – The Cure for Unbelief. Dake Study Bible Notes. Dakes Publishing. 1963.
[26] Fasting and Prayer – The Cure for Unbelief.

Fasting also releases power in us to overcome devils. We see that when Jesus overcame the devil in Matthew 4:1-11 and in the story of the epileptic boy's cure in Matthew 17:20-21.

This brief exegesis on fasting is to highlight its importance in the life of a believer, including the power to overcome strong spirits.

In earnestness, as you consider what you are dealing with, I ask you to come before the Lord in faith and humility and take a day to fast from food and pray. As you fast, a prayer guide is in the next section to guide you in praying liberating prayers. The foundational verses are listed at the end of the chapter for further meditation. Move into this next section when you are ready to fast.

Let us pray as we fast. Slowly read through each prayer. Pause to read through the scripture reference and speak it out loud before going on to the next prayer.

Prayer Guide

I. Entering into the gates of the Lord with thanksgiving and praise

Prayer: Lord, I thank You for Your word, which is a lamp unto my feet and a light unto my path. I know that through it all You are still God, and You are still good. In all things, I truly give You thanks. You deserve all the praise, and all the glory, and I honor You (Psalm 100:4).

II. Cleansing of the Lord

Prayer: Lord, according to Your Word, I submit myself before You that You cleanse me with Your blood. Wash me on the inside and the outside. Forgive me where I have sinned before You. Make me as white as snow, and purify my heart. As You stretch forth Your hand over me, I receive Your mercy, as You make me whole again (1 John 1:8–9).

III. Calling on the guidance and power of the Holy Spirit

Prayer: Lord, I pray for a fresh infilling of Your Holy Spirit. I need more of Your Holy Spirit to guide me and comfort me in this time. I ask for the power of the Holy Spirit to deliver me from every chain. Come, Holy Spirit (Romans 8:14–16).

IV. Binding the strongman

Prayer: Lord, I bind every strongman that stands guard over my soul, keeping me in the mires of negative emotions. Let

Your power deliver me from every such entity right now in Jesus's name (Romans 8:36).

V. The snare must be broken

Prayer: For every snare that I find myself in, I pray according to the Word of God that the snare be broken and my soul released. Every cage, every trap, every pit I have fallen into I renounce my spiritual connection to. I cry out to the Lord Jesus to break the snare. I declare: my soul is escaped in Jesus's name (Psalm 124:7–8).

VI. The curse must be reversed

Prayer: Every curse upon my life, upon my fathers and mothers before me, upon my spouse, upon my children, I declare broken in the name of Jesus. May the authority in the blood of Jesus break every curse and remove its effect on my life and family. Your power is above every power, and at the mention of Your name, every knee will bow. Right now, I ask that every curse upon me and my family bow and break, in the name of Jesus Christ (Philippians 4:9–11).

VII. Extraction and restoration of the soul

Prayer: Lord, destroy the stronghold of my soul and extract me from every ungodly pit. According to Your Word (2 Corinthians 10:3–5), our weapons of warfare have divine power to tear down strongholds. Right now, may every stronghold that I am entangled in be destroyed in Jesus's name. According to Your Word in Psalm 103:4, You redeem and extract our lives from the pit. Today, extract my soul from every pit. Redeem my soul from destruction. O Lord, restore my soul, in Jesus's name.

VIII. Healing

Prayer: Lord, heal the scars and mend the brokenness within. Stretch out Your arm and heal me, Lord. Bind my wounds and cure my inner ailments, in Jesus's name (Jeremiah 17:14, Jeremiah 33:6).

IX. Affirmation and thanksgiving

Lord, as the psalmist declared, we declare also: We have escaped like birds from the snare of the fowlers; the snare is broken, and we have escaped. Thank You for deliverance. Thank You for restoration. Thank You for Your faithfulness (Psalm 124:7).

Scriptures to continue in meditation after prayers

> Your word is a lamp to my feet and a light to my path. (Psalm 119:105)

> If we say that we have no sin, we deceive ourselves, and the truth is not in us. If we confess our sins, he who is faithful and just will forgive us our sins and cleanse us from all unrighteousness. (1 John 1:8–9)

> For all who are led by the Spirit of God are children of God. For you did not receive a spirit of slavery to fall back into fear, but you have received a spirit of adoption. When we cry, "Abba! Father!"

it is that very Spirit bearing witness with our spirit that we are children of God. (Romans 8:14–16)

We have escaped like a bird from the snare of the fowlers; the snare is broken, and we have escaped. Our help is in the name of the LORD, who made heaven and earth. (Psalms 124:7–8)

Who redeems your life from the Pit, who crowns you with steadfast love and mercy. (Psalms 103:4)

So if the Son makes you free, you will be free indeed. (John 8:36)

For the weapons of our warfare are not merely human, but they have divine power to destroy strongholds. We destroy arguments and every proud obstacle raised up against the knowledge of God, and we take every thought captive to obey Christ. (2 Corinthians 10:4–6)

So if anyone is in Christ, there is a new creation: everything old has passed away; see, everything has become new! (2 Corinthians 5:17)

Therefore God also highly exalted him and gave him the name that is above every name, so that at the name of Jesus every knee should bend, in heaven and on earth and under the earth, and every tongue should confess that Jesus Christ is Lord, to the glory of God the Father. (Philippians 2:9–11)

I am going to bring it recovery and healing; I will heal them and reveal to them abundance of prosperity and security. (Jeremiah 33:6)

Heal me, O LORD, and I shall be healed; Save me, and I shall be saved; for you are my praise. (Jeremiah 17:14)

MEDITATION AND PRAYER

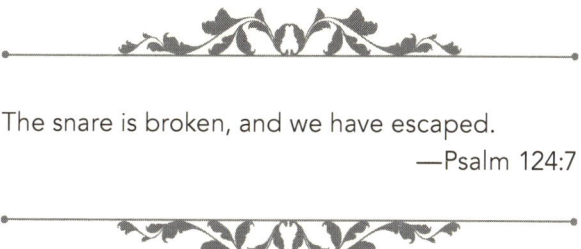

The snare is broken, and we have escaped.
—Psalm 124:7

Selah.

Pause and Meditate. Pause for a minute and take stock of your journey so far. These last two chapters with the prayer and fasting component began the liberation process from whatever was weighing your soul down.

Write: Journal your thoughts and experiences during the time of prayer and fasting. If you did not pray, I encourage you to pause and reread the chapter before continuing.

10

RESTORATION: LORD, RESTORE MY SOUL!

The LORD is my shepherd…he restores my soul.
—Psalm 23:1–3

ow that we have dealt with strongholds, we are positioned to embark on the path of restoration. Among the many attributes of God, God is a God of restoration. He rebuilds nations (Isaiah 62:4), restores health (Jeremiah 30:17), restores wealth (Jeremiah 32:15), and will cause you to recover wasted years.

Many words translate into *restore*. One such word is the Hebrew word *salaam*[27] as found in Joel 2:25: "I will restore (*salaam*) to you the years." Like many Hebrew words, *salaam*, carries within it a rich embodiment of meanings of restoration. Shining the light on each facet of this word-prism reveals a different aspect of restoration which serves

---

[27] ESV Strongs, #h7999 (Restore),

as its own blessing. May you experience *salaam* restorative blessings as we examine a few of these.

Salaam means to be made safe in mind, body, and estate. May the restoration of the Lord cause you to experience safety and soundness in your mind, soul, spirit, and body.

Salaam means to be complete. Where you were lost, where you were broken, where there was a void within you, may the restorative power of the Almighty God render you complete.

Salaam means to make amends. Where your brokenness caused schisms in various relationships, may God restore you and restore your relationships. May the grace to make amends, to walk in love, and to receive joy in fellowship be yours.

Salaam means peace and peaceable. Where you had no peace, may the Lord restore you in your inward being, so you begin to receive peace. May He restore your decision-making, thoughts, and actions, so you have both peace of mind, and be transformed into a person of peace.

Salaam means to be perfected. May the Lord perfect all that concerns you as He brings restoration to your soul. May He make your paths perfect, and may He guide you into His perfect will.

Salaam means prosperous. Receive the substantive restoration of the Lord. Receive prosperity in your soul, prosperity in your finances, health, and long life. May the richness of God's blessing rest upon you, leaving no residue of sorrow or heartache.

Yes, may you receive total restoration, in Jesus's name. The words of the Lord are life; receive them in faith. His

Word will build you up. His Word will heal you. Speak these words to your hearing, and declare them with faith over your life.

The following prayers are declarative restoration prayers to seal what God is initiating in your life in this season. Declare them in faith and boldness and receive restoration. May you be restored! May you be refreshed! May you be strengthened!

Prayers of Restoration

Prayer: May the Lord refresh my spirit, soul, and body. Create in me a clean heart, Lord, and renew my spirit, Lord. Restore to me joy. Where joy is gone from me, fill me afresh with Your joy. In Your presence, there is fullness of joy, and Your joy is my strength. I receive restoration of joy in my life as I pray. Thank You, Lord.

> Create in me a clean heart, O God, and put a new and right spirit within me. Do not cast me away from your presence, and do not take your holy spirit from me. Restore to me the joy of your salvation, and sustain in me a willing spirit. (Psalm 51:10–12)

Prayer: May the Lord restore all that has been taken from me: my zeal, my energy, my health, my vision for the kingdom, my intimacy with Him, and any other thing. May I be restored and made whole. The thief comes to kill, steal, and destroy. I pray for the end of the works of the thief in my life, and a sevenfold restoration in this season, in Jesus's name.

> Men do not despise a thief, if he steal to satisfy his soul when he is hungry; But if he be found, he shall restore sevenfold; he shall give all the substance of his house. (Proverbs 6:30–31 KJV)

Prayer: Lord, I thank You for the work You are doing in my life as I look to You for change. Help me to leave the things in the past as I walk in complete restoration. Thank You for the new thing You are doing in my life, expunging the old and the uncomely, and making a new way for me to walk in the beauty of destiny. As some of the paths seem unfamiliar and even challenging, grant me the grace to keep my eyes on You, to hold onto You in faith, knowing that You are the God who knows the plans He has for me—plans for a successful future. Thank you, Lord.

> Do not remember the former things, or consider the things of old. I am about to do a new thing; now it springs forth, do you not perceive it? I will make a way in the wilderness and rivers in the desert. (Isaiah 43:18–19)

Prayer: Lord, heal my unseen wounds. Heal the scars that I hide but that are very visible to me. Heal my heart and my mind. Where there are hurts and betrayal, let Your Word wash me, neutralizing the effect of the pain so I bear no grudge. Where I developed illnesses from the issues of life, I pray to You, Jehovah Rapha, to heal me. Stretch forth Your hand and restore me with Your healing power. I thank you in Jesus's name.

> For I will restore health to you, and your wounds I will heal, says the LORD, because they have called you an outcast: "It is Zion; no one cares for her!" (Jeremiah 30:17)

Prayer: Lord, restore the years and months that I seem to have wasted, the barren seasons where I bore no fruit and walked blindly. Restore those years unto me. May I recover all that I lost. May my mouth be satisfied once again because You, the Mighty Restorer, have lifted Your hand of favor over my life. I declare in accordance with Your Word that You are good, and You have dealt wondrously with me. Thank You, Lord.

> I will restore to you the years that the swarming locust has eaten, the hopper, the destroyer, and the cutter, my great army, which I sent among you. "You shall eat in plenty and be satisfied, and praise the name of the LORD your God, who has dealt wondrously with you. (Joel 2:25–26 ESV)

Prayer: Lord Almighty, I acknowledge that I am at fault, as I allowed different things to take hold of me. Restore me where I have fallen. Mend the brokenness in my soul. Like the words of the prayer You taught us to pray, lead me not into temptation, and deliver me from evil. Mend me and restore me in Jesus's name.

> My friends, if anyone is detected in a transgression, you who have received the Spirit should restore such a one in a spirit of gentleness. Take care that you yourselves are not tempted. (Galatians 6:1)

Prayer: Lord, where my hands have fallen short, doing everything but what You have called me to do, have mercy, and restore me. May these hands of mine bear much fruit, and may all that I put my hands to succeed because of the power of Your restoration. In Jesus's name.

> Then he said to the man, "Stretch out your hand." He stretched it out, and it was restored, as sound as the other. (Matthew 12:13)

Prayer: Lord, where my eyes have been blinded, and without vision and understanding, I place my hands on my eyes as I ask You to restore to me spiritual insight, foresight, and vision. I declare by the power that is in the name of Jesus, blessed are my eyes because they see and blessed are my ears because they hear (Matthew 13:16). I thank You for restoration.

> And the man looked up and said, "I can see people, but they look like trees, walking." Then Jesus laid his hands on his eyes again; and he looked intently and his sight was restored, and he saw everything clearly. (Mark 8:24–25)

Prayer: Lord, restore, mend, and heal my soul, and lead me on the right path once again. I thank You for hearing my cry, and I give You all the praise.

> He restores my soul. He leads me in right paths for his name's sake. (Psalms 23:3)

MEDITATION AND PRAYER

The LORD is my shepherd…he restores my soul.
—Psalm 23:1–3

Selah.

Pause and Meditate. Pause for a minute and take stock of your journey so far with these last chapters of prayer and meditation.

Write: Journal once again your thoughts and experiences during the time of prayer for restoration. You can repeat these prayers and declare these scriptures as often as you want to. There is power in the Word.

The subsequent chapters will deal with both practical and spiritual steps you can take to continue the journey of restoration and find rest for your soul in Christ.

11

RESTORATION: STEPPING OUT

This is the message we have heard from him and proclaim to you, that God is light and in him there is no darkness at all. If we say that we have fellowship with him while we are walking in darkness, we lie and do not do what is true; but if we walk in the light as he himself is in the light, we have fellowship with one another, and the blood of Jesus his Son cleanses us from all sin. If we say that we have no sin, we deceive ourselves, and the truth is not in us. If we confess our sins, he who is faithful and just will forgive us our sins and cleanse us from all unrighteousness. If we say that we have not sinned, we make him a liar, and his word is not in us.

—1 John 1:5–10

Again, liberation is possible! You have taken the significant step of prayer and you have identified areas where repentance is needed. The next big step is transitioning out of what is past and stepping into your new phase. The 1 John 1 pericope of scripture gives us some guidance on this.

Step One: Choose to step out

Verse 5 says in God there is no darkness—at all. That's powerful ideology. Following Christ means where there is darkness lurking, you make a conscious decision to step away from it, even though it may seem impossible. This involves both your will and your prayer. Where there is addiction involved, this step may also involve willingness to see a counselor or therapist. Having trusted individuals praying with and for you is also helpful in this step for both support and accountability. In the case of substance use, a licensed clinician or facility will be needed to monitor withdrawal symptoms, which can be fatal in some cases. However, the decision to step out takes you halfway there.

Step Two: Name it and speak it out

The scripture says *if we confess our sins*, God is faithful and will not only forgive but *cleanse us from all unrighteousness*. To be cleansed of unrighteousness is to deal with the source that causes habitual unrighteous thoughts, acts, and deeds. God already knows your constitution, struggles, pain, guilt, and situation. Your confession acknowledges to yourself that it doesn't belong with you, and also that you need help beyond yourself. The name El Shaddai is a rich name of God that can be interpreted as the Double-Breasted One.

Another derived meaning is the One who can do for you what you cannot do for yourself. Your confession activates El Shaddai to begin to intervene in a special way. You stay in darkness longer when you don't come face to face with it and call it by its real name: sin, darkness, depression, self-pity, resentment, doubt, hurt, wrongdoing, or addiction. Whatever it is, confession starts the journey.

Step Three: Find a partner or partners

The 1 John scripture further exhorts that *we have fellowship with one another.* Find people you can associate with on this new journey and one or two people you will be accountable to. You can choose to share your challenges with them, or simply decide that you want a closer association with them because of their positive influence. This is fellowshipping in the light. Out the door go the people who seduce your weaker self, and in come those who are sheer positivity and encouragement.

Quickly going back to the discussion of dopamine and the brain, there are times when interaction with a person associated with your previous struggle can create a desire for you to resume the negative behavior again. Distancing from such people helps achieve a new normal, and finding trustworthy individuals to journey with is pivotal. This is not to be done without caution, however. Placing the right people around you does not mean you use them as a standard of perfection. You may have been there when you were someone's rod of perfection and you disliked it because you knew you were not without your faults.

This cautionary approach is necessary in the event you are exposed to the person's cracks and faults. It prevents you from falling alongside them as feelings of disillusionment, betrayal, and even despair kick in.

Everyone, without exception, needs the grace of God to fulfill his or her destiny and to walk this journey. That's why the verse says, "If we say that we have not sinned, we make him a liar, and his word is not in us." Some may be more mature and able to lead and guide others amid their own pain and issues. That, however, does not put them outside of the reach of the very things *you* are dealing with. Surround yourself with people who are in the light, but do not put them on infallible pedestals. When you see them crack, let it encourage you that you are not alone in your struggles. That should help you give them grace in their times of need.

Step Four: Keep the past behind you

There is nothing more demoralizing than seeing your past failures and issues flashing before you. It has the power to cripple you and deter you from moving forward. The enemy of your soul loves to keep bringing up the past to confuse your present. What the Lord does in your life, however, is *now*. He forgives you in the present and says, "I will not remember your sins" (Isaiah 43:25). He cleanses you in the present, so that what happened yesterday is gone. Even your achievements of the past should be kept safely in the past so as not to create complacency in the present. As long as you remain in this mortal body, you will have to keep striving for perfection. Assume the mantra of Apostle Paul:

> Beloved, I do not consider that I have made it my own; but this one thing I do: forgetting what lies behind and straining forward to what lies ahead. (Philippians 3:13)

Keep the past behind you, and step into a new season with boldness and confidence knowing that God is already working things together for your good.

Step Five: Partner with the Word

The Word of God is living, active, and strengthening. It is the truth we need. It fills the vacuum left by grieving, loss, and erroneous choices. The Word is light in our darkness. The Word in us is Christ in us. We have to decide to abide in the Word and let the Word, in turn, abide in us. Our soul needs the Word, and a separation from it is the one thing that can weaken and burden the soul.

Back to James 1:21, which states, "Welcome with meekness the implanted word that has the power to save your souls." The Word has the power to restore the brokenness within the soul. Remember, the soul is the bridge between the spiritual and the physical realms. Every single day, we are bombarded with unsuitable images, presented with ungodly feelings and attitudes, and given opportunity to be resentful, to doubt, to have low self-esteem, amid a host of projections from external sources. Engaging in the Word strengthens the soul to be an effective filter, filtering out the negativity received from all the bombarding. This happens partly through the cleansing action of the Word of God. The opening verse talks about the Lord *cleansing* us of all our unrighteousness. This happens hand in hand with repentance. As we confess our faults, and partner with the Word, it begins to cleanse us on the inside. Our hearts and spirits, in turn, do not receive the full strength of the bombardment. The Word strengthens that filter of the soul as it cleanses us.

Separation from the Word weakens that filter and cuts off the cleansing that happens, similar to a clogged drain. The farther you are from fellowship with the Word, the less firm your conscience, and the less convicted you are to devoting yourself unto a godly life. When that soul filter is restored through the Word, its impact is seen in our spiritual walk and even in the health of our entire being.

> My child, be attentive to my words; incline your ear to my sayings. Do not let them escape from your sight; keep them within your heart. For they are life to those who find them, and healing to all their flesh. (Proverbs 4:20–22)

The Word not only restores us, but gives us life, and brings healing to our flesh. We, in turn, need to make a commitment to renew our vows with the Word of God, not unlike the vows to a marriage partner.

Not straying from the words of the verse, let us look at four ways to partner with the Word to aid our restoration processes. First, we need to be attentive to the Word. This implies that we need to prioritize our activities to intentionally include the reading of the Word and be attentive to its message for each day. Look at your schedule and build in time for the Word of God.

Second, our ears have to be inclined to hear, receive, and obey the Word in the different forms that it comes to us. The hearing happens when we open our spirits to what God is saying through His Word, while developing the habit of speaking it out loud back to ourselves.

Third, the Word has to be kept within our sights, which suggests going beyond simply reading into memorization. In that way, we can "see" it in our hearts and minds even when our Bibles are not physically open. These are actions we have to decide to pursue.

Finally, the verse talks about keeping the Word in our hearts, which involves meditation on the chosen scripture, believing in what the scripture promises, and focusing on the light it imparts rather than the darkness around us. That way, the heart of the message dwells with us long after the physical book is closed. God says, "For surely I know the plans I have for you, says the LORD, plans for your welfare and not for harm, to give you a future with hope" (Jeremiah 29:11). No matter what is happening in our lives, we must keep our hearts and minds steadily on the hope and thought that God has better plans ahead.

As we continue in these steps, we start to notice an exchange happening.

> Come to me, all you that are weary and are carrying heavy burdens, and I will give you rest. Take my yoke upon you, and learn from me; for I am gentle and humble in heart, and you will find rest for your souls. For my yoke is easy, and my burden is light. (Matthew 11:28–20)

The divine exchange, as you come to Him, begins to be actualized. Your heavy burden and weariness start to dissipate and you begin to experience rest for your soul. You find yourself carrying a lighter burden and bearing an easier yoke.

MEDITATION AND PRAYER

Who redeems your life from the Pit, who crowns you with steadfast love and mercy.

—Psalm 103:4

Selah.

Pause and Meditate. Which of the steps do you need to apply? What do you need to put in place to begin? I suggest that you start some type of journaling process to keep yourself accountable.

Pray with me: Lord, You are light and life. I choose to step out of the pit I am in and release myself into Your hands. Fix me where I am broken. Renew my desire for Your Word. Surround me with divinely appointed partners. I thank You for a new beginning, in Jesus's name. Amen.

12

RESTORATION: THE FIGHT

Fight the good fight of the faith; take hold of the
eternal life, to which you were called and for which
you made the good confession in the presence of
many witnesses.

—1 Timothy 6:12

Your journey of walking in the rest Jesus promises
is a continuous fight. An oxymoron indeed, but
also the truth. Once you walk in freedom from
snares, you need to fight to stay in that state. Staying free is
about fighting the good fight every day. The battle between
darkness and light, between liberation and bondage, is
intense and must be fought with intentionality. When you
begin the journey of coming out of darkness, you will find
that the beginning is the most difficult time because the
darkness does not want to let you go. The one saying no to
drinking will have intense cravings for alcohol, almost to the
point where the person feels he or she will die without it.
The mind immediately says, "No need for this withdrawal.

Let's just go for it." That's why it's important to be in an environment free of alcohol in such a case (a strong clinical recommendation).

The mind says to call that person who is toxic to your soul one more time, to numb your senses so you don't feel the anxiety and pain just one more time. This is when being surrounded by friends and partners who support your new endeavor helps. When all the energy to restrain yourself is gone, the presence or the knowledge of that person becomes motivation to not break your resolution. Whether it's prescription or recreational drugs, or sexual addictions, make the sacrificial effort to remove yourself from the environment of the temptation. That does not mean you still will not be tempted. It means that you have created a barrier to make the temptation less accessible.

Staying free and in the light is a fight. Now that the body and soul are rejecting the darkness, the forces of darkness play on the mind. They remind you of the pleasures of indulging, of the "great" times, of how you could have temporary pleasure if you could go back for even just a minute. You have to intentionally turn off those suggestions, physically engage in an activity or hobby, or call your accountability partner to combat the feelings of despair that those suggestions bring up.

Fight through prayer

Jesus prayed, "Lead us not into temptation" (Matthew 6:13 ESV). In the light of what we have covered so far, this prayer is especially meaningful to pray alongside the steps you are taking. Pray for yourself and ask your trustworthy prayer partner to pray with you. Pray that the temptation and desire be dried out.

Jesus also prayed, "Deliver us from evil" (Matthew 6:13 ESV). This prayer recognizes the role that evil powers play in our lives and teaches us to call on God's power to deliver us. This severs the lingering hold of darkness on your mind.

Freedom is not only in not partaking of the temptation but also in not having to think about how much you desire to. The mind can be transformed to reject both the temptation and the thought of it. It takes the power of God for such an absolute turn, and it is one hundred percent possible. Does it mean you will not fall? You probably will. However, never give up the act of getting up and moving on, not looking back, and not wallowing in the depression that can overwhelm you after falling. Just keep marching on like a soldier. Never give up simply because you stumbled. You have more strength than you think. Keep moving on every single day.

Fight through the daily reset mindset

> And he said to all, "If anyone would come after me, let him deny himself and take up his cross daily and follow me." (Luke 9:23 ESV)

Take each new day as a new beginning. Here are four things you can do to officially start your day in forty seconds. First, find and celebrate a victory from yesterday, including the fact that you are alive to experience a new day. Speak aloud things you are grateful for. The attitude of gratitude helps shape your perspective. Second, speak a positive confession over your day, for example, "Today, I will do well and have positive experiences." Third, state a goal for the day, such as, "Today I will not overeat." Fourth, turn your eyes on Jesus. It can be through a simple statement, like "Lord Jesus, my eyes are on You. Help me through today." On the next day's reset, thank Him for helping you through the previous day.

If the failure of yesterday is trying to weigh you down, admit you fell, pray for strength for a new day, and reset. The power of starting afresh each day is the power of the reset. The book of Proverbs gives us glimpses into deep wisdom keys. We learn that "For the righteous falls seven times and rises again, but the wicked stumble in times of calamity" (Proverbs 24:16 ESV). The fall is not unexpected. However, our attitudes toward that should not be of self-pity and depression. On the contrary, we should think, *I have the capacity to rise again, and I will.*

Reset every new day, and do so again with these practical tenets grounded in the Luke 9:23 verse above. Reset by stating your goal. Reset each day by choosing to deny yourself for that day as old desires arise. Reset by taking up your cross daily. Reset by making a choice to follow Jesus daily.

Fight with the Word of God

> Take my yoke upon you, and learn from me; for I am gentle and humble in heart, and you will find rest for your souls. (Matthew 11:29)

Pick up your Bible, and begin to slowly go through it. Jesus said, "Learn of me." This is simple, yet hard to practice.

Read and study His Word. Live by His principles. Learn of Him.

Fight with Fasting

> And whenever you fast, do not look dismal, like the hypocrites, for they disfigure their faces so as to show others that they are fasting. Truly I tell you, they have received their reward. But when you fast, put oil on your head and wash your face, so that your fasting may be seen not by others but by your Father who is in secret; and your Father who sees in secret will reward you. (Matthew 6:16–18)

Add regular times of fasting to your arsenal. Fasting draws us closer to God because we subdue the flesh and allow the spirit to minister to God, who is a spirit. Jesus, who said "when" you fast (taking the optionality out), also talks about reward. There is a reward when you fast. The reward could be in many forms, including keeping the world of darkness and temptation away from you and your house, a closer walk with God, uniquely answered prayers, and the power to overcome various challenges. Fight to maintain your new season through intentional fasts.

MEDITATION AND PRAYER

Blessed be the LORD, my rock, who trains my hands for war, and my fingers for battle.

—Psalm 144:1

Selah.

Pause and Meditate. You have come this far—congratulations! Assess yourself and see where you need to focus or refocus and keep fighting the good fight. God is on your side.

Pray with me: Lord, I thank you for Your plans for me, plans of good and not evil. Thank You for greater things that are ahead. Thank You for Your grace that is enabling me to keep moving forward and to keep fighting. Thank You for restoration. All glory and honor belong to You. In Jesus's name. Amen.

13

PHYSICAL WELL-BEING: START SOMEWHERE

Beloved, I pray that you may prosper in all things and be in health, just as your soul prospers.
—3 John1:2 (NKJV)

The Lord is interested in the wellness of your whole being. Restoration encompasses everything that concerns you. The Lord is interested in every part of your life. This includes your body being healthy (1 Thessalonians 5:23, 3 John 1:2), your mind being sound (2 Timothy 1:7), your finances being in good order, your soul prospering (3 John 1:2), and your spirit being bound for eternity. We've delved into the soul and will now switch focus to briefly touch on physical well-being and spiritual well-being.

Physical Wellness: Start Somewhere.

Eat Well

Start somewhere. We all know what balanced diets are, what eating late does to our bodies, and why we need to drink more water. Knowing and doing are sometimes on different planes. Give yourself a small goal to start with. It could be as simple as cutting down on sodas and drinking more water. It could be setting a goal to not eat after 7 p.m. Carve time in your day to eat a good meal wherever you are so you do not come home at night to eat just before going to bed.

Medical Wellness Checks

Start somewhere. At least have an annual wellness check with your doctor. In each season, the care is different. When you are under forty without malaises, these should be routine, performed at least once a year. Once you cross the forty line, mammograms, prostrate checks, and the like become important. Don't wait until you cannot be helped before finding a doctor because you were "too busy taking care of this other thing."

Exercise

Start somewhere. Yes, we know that cardiovascular health is dependent on exercises like walking, jogging, and so on. We also know that strength training helps to keep the body in good shape. Again, knowing and doing have a chasm between them. We have gym memberships that go unused. We keep talking about the last time we did vigorous exercise and how we will be going back (it's been six years now). Start somewhere. Walk fifteen to twenty minutes a day during the evening, or during the morning, or any time when your mind will not find an excuse. Build from there.

Engage

Start somewhere. Engage with your family. Have lunch together on Saturdays. Fast together. Re-engage with your friends who you left behind because you were too busy. Pick up the phone and check on them. Spend time with the people who are close to you. It can be frustrating for your family to see how much time you spend with that person who needs help, the overseer who calls you seven times a day, and the person who calls you three times with the same question, but yet have no time for them. Your spouse, your immediate family, and your close friends are like plants that need the water of your attention and engagement. Don't deprive them of it.

Also, engage or build a peer group of people in your vocation or office. It does not need to be a lot of people. Two is more than enough. It gets lonely in some vocations, especially when you start speaking the language of that vocation. Don't trudge through alone.

Financial Wellness Check

Start somewhere. The National Association of Evangelicals (NAE), in 2016, studied 4,249 ministers across nineteen denominations in the United States regarding their finances. Here are some of their findings.

- 50 percent receive compensation of less than $50,000 per year, with 30 percent having student loan debt averaging $36,000.
- 33 percent had retirement funds under $10,000.
- 29 percent had no personal savings.
- 25 percent had medical bills averaging $7,253.00.[28]

These statistics may strike a chord with you, or you may have your finances all set. If you are not all set, start somewhere.

Have a savings plan for you and your family if you have a family. If not, start one for yourself. Have a plan for retirement. It is never too late to start. Spend cautiously. Give generously. John Wesley preached a sermon called "The Use of Money." In it, he shared that people should earn

---

[28] NAE. Majority of Pastors Suffer in Silence over Financial Challenges. www.nae.org/pastorresearch.

all they can, then save all they can, and give all they can.[29] This resource has a lot of good principles to consider. Write a will or consult with an estate planner or medical director so that when you transition to your heavenly mansion, those left behind do not have to add financial stress to their grief. Your estate legacy plans do not evolve "naturally," so spell them out in a will or estate plan. Resources and contact information are at the end of the book if you need a starting point. Reach out by all means, but don't do nothing.

Find a Hobby (Coping Mechanism Alternative)

The lack of intentional cultivation of a hobby was probably most glaring during the pandemic. With no commute time, almost no in-person meetings, less interaction, and less errand running, people suddenly had time on their hands they did not have previously. Some were overwhelmed with having too much time and started running into excesses. Others cultivated beautiful gardens, built furniture, painted, restored old upholstery, and so on. Others pursued certifications and courses, some caught up on reading, some started to write or draw or sew. When that soul issue you have gotten rid of comes knocking on your door again, in addition to spiritual mechanisms such as prayer that you put in place, have a hobby that will kill the time you would have had to indulge in those triggers.

---

[29] John Wesley. The Use of Money. https://nbc.whdl.org/sites/default/files/resource/book/ EN_John_Wesley_050_use_of_money .htm

MEDITATION AND PRAYER

Search me, O God, and know my heart; test me and know my thoughts.

—Psalm 139:23

Selah.

Pause and Meditate. How did you fare during the physical wellness check? Do you recognize opportunities for change? What has been the greatest inhibitor to starting a new physical routine? How best do you think you can overcome this?

Pray with me: Lord, I thank You for life and how precious it is. Help me to be a good steward of the very life You have given me by taking steps to care for my being. I ask Lord, please heal my ailments, prolong my days, and add Your blessing to my efforts. Amen.

14

SPIRITUAL WELL-BEING: A QUICK CHECK-UP

May the God of peace himself sanctify you entirely; and may your spirit and soul and body be kept sound and blameless at the coming of our Lord Jesus Christ.

—1 Thessalonians 5:23

The saddest phenomenon is seeing a minister who preaches powerfully because he has prepared extensively, but has no personal devotional time or real relationship with the Lord. You are good and conscientious, but you are also in danger of not feeding your spirit as you feed your constituents. Your prowess must not only be exercised on the outside. Undergirding the outward ministration must be the conscientious exercising of spiritual discipline in your life. Let us consider a few things when conducting a wellness check on our spirit being.

Daily time spent with the Lord

This is time you intentionally put aside to spend with the Lord. It is alone time with Him, your Bible, and whatever helps you create an atmosphere of intimacy with Him. It is the deliberate development of your relationship with Him by getting to know Him and learning to wait on Him. This is how we are refreshed daily. We breathe Him in and exhale the stresses and pressures of this world. Developing the discipline of spending time daily with the Lord has two important side effects. I call them side effects because they are not the ultimate goal. The first is that when you don't feel like doing so due to fatigue, discouragement, and the like, the discipline of coming before the Lord will sustain you in those times. This very act of spending time with the Lord will bring you out of the pit. The second side effect is that in times of crisis, it will be your go-to instead of the mind-numbing indulgences you would naturally turn to, which make the issue worse. How much time do you dedicate to time alone with Him? What initial goal can you set to begin to enact material changes in your life?

Studying His Word

This also is time you set aside to delve into His Word to build yourself up and to know Him more. My challenge still stands: look deeply into scriptures that you come across and mine them for the gold they contain. Psalm 119 has 176 benefits (yes, not an error) of studying God's word.

Verse 18 says that we will begin to see wonderful things he reveals to us. Verse 28 states that we will be strengthened. Verse 36 says that we will be less inclined to turn to selfish gain when tempted. Verse 98 states that we may become wiser than our enemies and outwit them. Verse 99 says we may develop more understanding than those who have taught us in the past, or even have more understanding than the "ancients" (verse 100). Verse 176 tells us we will be re-routed onto the right path when we start to stray and become lost. The list goes on.

There is power in studying the Word of God. There is also power in committing various scriptures to memory so the Word is alive in you and becomes the backing authority of your decrees and professions. Studying the Word will additionally lend uncommon soundness to your thinking. It makes you spiritual. How much of your non-teaching and non-preaching time are you dedicating to personal study? What goal can you set to change the course?

Times of prayer

No statistics are needed to measure the lack of average prayer time of ministers. Some are too busy to pray, some believe five minutes of prayer a day is enough, and some don't see the value of prayer. The late David Yonggi Cho, who had the largest church in Asia, said, "You must take the time to pray to the Lord, even though you neglect the work of God. It is essential that you first serve God in prayer."[30] In this highly recommended read, he provides several instances when he chose prayer over ministering and prevented burnout. I have listed some of Cho's resources at the end of the book if this article stirred something in you. Jesus rose a great while before day to find a solitary place to pray before His day started (Mark 1:35). If the Son of God is modeling prayer before us, let us learn of Him and do the same. I have compiled some prayers in my book *Fire on the Prayer Altar* to guide you if you need a prayer starter pack.

Engaging the Holy Spirit

"For as many as are led by the Spirit of God, these are sons of God" (Romans 8:14 NKJV). That's you and me. When we learn to take the Holy Spirit on as our partner, praying for His direction, leading, guidance, and empowerment, we are truly sons and daughters of God. Pray for the Holy Spirit, and pray in the Holy Spirit. Pray for the guidance of the Holy Spirit. Pray for the anointing of the Holy Spirit. Pray for the power of the Holy Spirit in your life and ministry. Listen to His promptings. Heed His warnings. In doing this, we are not only setting ourselves up for success, we are delivering ourselves from a lot of heartache as well. This is not to say that life will be perfect, but our resilience, reactions, decisions, and actions in the face of challenges will be different.

---

[30] David Yonggi Cho. Why I pray so much. https://prevailinggrace. wordpress.com/2015/12/27/why-i-pray-so-much-2/

Iron Sharpens Iron

"Iron sharpens iron, and one person sharpens the wits of another" (Proverbs 27:17). Keep those who value relationship with the Lord close to your heart. They may not always be those in service of the house of God. Ananias, who prayed for the apostle Paul to regain his sight, was not known for his title or his church but simply as a disciple with whom the Lord spoke (Acts 9:10–12). Find an Ananias in your life who challenges you to grow closer to Christ, to be sensitive to His calling and instruction, and who will challenge you to live a life of devotion to Christ.

Develop Healthy Boundaries

> Everything is permissible (allowable and lawful) for me; but not all things are helpful (good for me to do, expedient and profitable when considered with other things). Everything is lawful for me, but I will not become the slave of anything or be brought under its power. (1 Corinthians 6:12 AMP)

This verse strikes the balance between creating boundaries for the sake of Christ without becoming religious and legalistic. All things are *permissible* or, as the KJV says, all things are *lawful*. No one is preventing you from going to Hooters, or the casinos, or into the bedroom of someone of the opposite sex alone. Many antagonists would ask where it is written in the Bible that they cannot gamble. The second part of the scripture sheds light without the legalistic shade: *it is permissible,* but first, *it is not helpful to me,* and second, *I will not be brought under the power of anything.* Develop healthy boundaries in your relationships with people, especially those who drain you. Develop healthy boundaries with your constituent members. Develop healthy boundaries around the opposite sex. Develop healthy boundaries regarding food and fasting. Develop healthy boundaries on what you would not compromise on. Learn to say "no" and understand that the price of your "yes" is sometimes too high for your well-being.

Speak Life

A stunning illustration of the impact of what one utters is seen in Numbers 28:14. The Lord had given the Israelites land and sent them to survey the gift He had given them. When the surveying committee went, some saw the beauty and the potential of the land. Others saw the literal giants and beasts, and the struggle that lay ahead if they possessed the land. Out of what they saw, they respectively declared from their hearts. Joshua and Caleb were excited and declared, "Let us go up at once and occupy it, for we are well able to overcome it" (Numbers 13:30). The others, in their intimidation, declared, "We are not able to go up against this people, for they are stronger than we...Would that we had died in the land of Egypt! Or would that we had died in this wilderness!" (Numbers 13:31, 14:2).

This enraged the Lord, who had performed many miracles before them. The plagues of Egypt had played before their eyes. The Red Sea was parted for them and their families to pass through, delivering them from the evil machinations of Pharaoh. In the face of God's promise for the land, all they could see was the negatives. Note that God responded to them by saying, "As I live...I will do to you the very things I heard you say: your dead bodies shall fall in this very wilderness" (Numbers 14:28–29b). The story was very different for Joshua and Caleb, who agreed verbally with the Lord despite what they saw. Speak life. Speak the promises of God. Speak the hope of God. He notes what we say, and He gives us what we profess.

> Death and life are in the power of the tongue, and
> those who love it will eat its fruits. (Proverbs 18:21)

The Lord is not a man that He should lie. Hold fast to His promises and repeat them to yourself in your hearing and the hearing of the Lord. Listen to your thoughts and words as the day goes along and make sure that you are speaking life.

Read, Listen, Immerse

"Buy truth, and do not sell it; buy wisdom, instruction, and understanding" (Proverbs 23:23). "Grow in the grace and knowledge of our Lord and Savior Jesus Christ" (2 Peter 3:18). It's nice to have everyone comment on your library, but it is far more helpful to read the books. Develop a love for reading sound material that will help you grow. Seek enriching materials and invest in them. It ends up being an investment for your soul. Two ways to ease into reading if it is tough for you is to get the audiobook version of the book or approach it as a devotional. The audiobook reads for you as you do mundane things like driving and other activities that consume what I refer to as "white spaces" of time in your day. You either use that time to think, listen to the news, or find yourself in the wrong thinking space. They are chunks of time that are not short enough to be immaterial, but also not long enough to have a more actionable plan. Those "white spaces" of time are great for pressing "play" on that audiobook.

The other strategy of reading it as a devotional takes away the pressure of needing to finish a whole book now. You can take three to four pages a day as you wait on God, or whatever time works for you to learn something that will edify your spirit. You glean more nuggets that way. Whatever strategy you choose is up to you, as long as you start the art of having a book you are always reading to sharpen the spiritual person within you.

Immerse yourself in listening to sound teaching. The addition of the word "sound" is deliberate. How do you tell what is "sound"? Unfortunately, denominational boundaries and perspectives have started to redefine what soundness should be. If the things written are in agreement with the denominational statement of faith, it's good, and if they are not, it's not sound. However, the word of God is inexhaustible. It cannot be defined by denominational appetites. In Psalm 119:80 (KJV), David prays, "Let my heart be sound in thy statutes; that I be not ashamed." The Hebrew word used is *tâmîym*, translated by Strong's as "without blemish, complete, perfect, full, sincerely, and whole."[31] Soundness implies making all effort with the help of the Holy Spirit to present or teach the scripture in its complete, full, and whole form from a sincere heart. Because the Holy Spirit was a "co-writer" of the scriptures (2 Peter 1:20–21), He will help you discern what is sound, irrespective of denominational coloring. Nevertheless, find sound teaching and be inspired and stirred up as you feed your soul.

---

[31] KJV Strong's Dictionary. #h8549

MEDITATION AND PRAYER

Search me, O God, and know my heart; test me and know my thoughts.

—Psalm 139:23

Selah.

Pause and Meditate. How did you fare during the spiritual check-up? Do you recognize opportunities for personal growth? What struck you the most?

Pray with me: Lord, I thank You for how far You have brought me. Grant me the grace to go even further. Help me become more spiritual, as I learn to become more like You. Grant me the desire to study Your Word, to spend time with You in prayer, as You teach me Your ways. Open my eyes unto deeper understanding and immerse me in Your love. In Jesus's name. Amen.

15

REST FOR YOUR SOUL. A FINAL WORD

Come to Me, all you who labor and are heavy-laden and overburdened, and I will cause you to rest. [I will ease and relieve and refresh your souls.] Take My yoke upon you and learn of Me, for I am gentle (meek) and humble (lowly) in heart, and you will find rest (relief and ease and refreshment and recreation and blessed quiet) for your souls.

—Matthew 11:28–29 (AMP)

I commend you for sticking with it to the end. Knowledge is the beginning of any undertaking. Apply this knowledge consistently and take steps to find that blessed rest. Allow healing to run its course in your life. Take severe measures to cut off toxic habits and toxic relationships in your sphere. You may need to take some time off to regroup. It may be time to transition into something new. You may need to examine what has been your routine for the last decade or two and start finding small opportunities to implement change. One change could be a daily devotional time with the Lord. You may even need to find conferences outside of your normal circles, where you purposefully attend to receive and be refreshed.

Learn *of* Jesus daily. Learn *from* Jesus daily—not for your congregation, but for you. Give Him your burden and take His yoke, so that you find physical and spiritual strength and rest for your soul and can be an overcomer in this next phase of your life.

This is not the end for you, but the beginning of a new season. Jesus said if anyone thirsts, he should come and drink (John 7:37). Drink deep of Him. As you drink of him, you will be refreshed and refilled with spiritual waters of refreshment. Moreover, you will be able to water others because in drinking yourself, your belly will flow with rivers of living water (John 7:38), with which you will bless many others. You will find yourself a more effective leader, a more effective minister, and a more fruitful individual.

Pray with me. Lord, thank You for Your care for me, which supersedes the care of any person. I come humbly to You, to learn of You. Restore my soul, Lord. Restore to me the joy of knowing You. Restore to me the joy of salvation. Restore to me the joy of serving You. In Jesus's name. Amen.

May the Lord release his blessing on you!

I WANT TO HEAR
FROM YOU

The best part about writing this book was the times of prayer and promptings of the Holy Spirit. I prayed for you many times. I would like to hear from you. Whether it's just a comment, a question, or a desire to pursue a subject I simply touched on, reach out. If you even want to set up an appointment for someone to pray with, reach out. You are not alone in what you are dealing with, or where you are. susan.agbenoto@gmail.com.

BIBLIOGRAPHY

Bellini, Peter J. "Truth Therapy: Renewing Your Mind with the Word of God." Wipf and Stock Publishers, 2014.

Berridge, Kent C. and Morten L. Kringelbach. "Pleasure systems in the brain." Neuron 86, no. 3 (2015): 646–664.

Cho, David Yonggi. "Why I Pray So Much." https://prevailinggrace. wordpress.com/2015/12/27/why-i-pray-so-much-2/

Duplantis, Jesse. "I never learned to doubt." Destrehan, LA: Jesse Duplantis, 2022.

Hagin, Kenneth. How You Can Be Led by the Spirit of God. Tulsa, OK: Faith Library Publications, 2008.

Krejcir, Richard J. PIR Ministries. "Statistics on Pastors." Accessed November 23, 2023. https://pirministries.org/wp-content/uploads/2016/01/FASICLD-Statistics-on-Pastors.pdf

Lee, Witness. The Soul having three parts. http://www.ministrysamples.org/excerpts/THE-SOUL-HAVINGTHREE-PARTS.HTML Smith, Winston T. Burned Out? Trusting God with Your "To-Do" List. Greensboro, NC: New Growth Press, 2010

Lembke, Anna. Dopamine Nation: Finding Balance in the Age of Indulgence. New York: Penguin Publishing Group, 2021.

NAE. "Majority of Pastors Suffer in Silence over Financial Challenges." Accessed December 12, 2023. www.nae.org/pastorresearch.

Pasnau, Robert. "Thomas Aquinas," in The Stanford Encyclopedia of Philosophy (Spring 2023 Edition), ed. Edward N. Zalta and Uri Nodelman, accessed November 20, 2023, https://plato.stanford.edu/archives/spr2023/entries/aquinas.

Pastoral Care Inc. Accessed November 19, 2023. www.pastoralcareinc.com/statistics.

Powledge, Tabitha M. "Addiction and the brain: The dopamine pathway is helping researchers find their way through the addiction maze," BioScience, Volume 49, Issue 7, July 1999.

Prince, Derek. "Resurrection!" Posted April 12, 2013. YouTube video, 50:48. https://www.youtube.com/watch?v=DiyDrwwiU6E.

Robinson, Terry E., and Bryan Kolb. "Structural plasticity associated with exposure to drugs of abuse." Neuropharmacology 47 (2004).

Thomistic Philosophy. "Body and Soul," Accessed November 20, 2023, https://aquinasonline.com/body-and-soul.

Wellness Universe. "What is Spiritual Wellness?" Wellness Universe. Accessed November 20, 2023. https://blog.thewellnessuniverse.com/top-2-spiritual-wellnessresources/.

Wesley, John. The Use of Money. https://nbc.whdl.org/sites/default/files/resource/book/EN John Wesley 050 use of money.htm

RESOURCES

Recommended Readings and Catalog of References

Engaging the Holy Spirit

Hagin, Kenneth. How You Can Be Led by the Spirit of God. Tulsa, OK: Faith Library Publications, 2008.

Heward-Mills, Dag. Sweet Influences of the Anointing. Accra: Parchment House, 2018.

Theology 101

Grudem, Wayne A. Christian Beliefs: 20 Basics Every Christian Should Know. Zondervan, 2005.

The Stanford Encyclopedia of Philosophy (Spring 2023 Edition), s.v. "Thomas Aquinas" by Robert Pasnau, accessed November 20, 2023, https://plato.stanford.edu/archives/spr2023/entries/aquinas.

Prince, Derek. Foundational Truths for Christian Living: Everything You Need to Know to Live a Balanced, Spirit-Filled Life. Lake Mary, FL: Charisma Media, 2006.

Deliverance 101

Clark, Randy. The Biblical Guidebook to Deliverance. Lake Mary, FL: Charisma Media, 2015.

Bottari, Paolo. Free in Christ. Lake Mary, FL: Charisma Media, 2000.

Prayer

Agbenoto, Susan. Fire on the Prayer Altar, (pre-release, 2024)

Cho, David Yonggi. Prayer That Brings Revival. Lake Mary, FL: Charisma House, 1998.

Cho, David Yonggi, and R. Whitney Manzano. The Fourth Dimension. Vol. 2. Newberry, FL: Bridge Logos Foundation, 1979.

Cho, David Yonggi. Why I Pray So Much. https://prevailinggrace.wordpress.com/2015/12/27/why-i-pray-so-much-2/

Eckhardt, John. Prayers that route Demons. Lake Mary Florida: Charisma House, 2017.

Picardo, Rosario and Sue Nelson Kibbey. Dynamite Prayer. Plano, Texas: Invite Press, 2022.

Keating, Thomas. Open mind, Open heart: The contemplative dimension of the gospel. A&C Black, 2002.

Life in the Spirit and Practical Christianity

Agbenoto, Susan. New Wine. (Pre-release, Christian Faith Publishers, 2024)

Bellini, Peter J. Truth Therapy: Renewing Your Mind with the Word of God. Wipf and Stock Publishers, 2014.

Duplantis, Jesse. I Never Learned to Doubt. Destrehan, LA: Jesse Duplantis, 2022.

Lee, Witness. The Soul having three parts. http://www.ministrysamples.org/excerpts/THE-SOUL-HAVING-THREE-PARTS.HTML Smith, Winston T. Burned Out? Trusting God with Your "To-Do" List. Greensboro, NC: New Growth Press, 2010

Smith, Winston T. Divorce Recovery. Growing and Healing God's Way. Greensboro, NC: New Growth Press, 2008

Financial Well-Being

Picardo, Callie and Rosario Picardo. Money Talks. Knoxville, Tennessee: Market Square Publishing LLC, 2021.

Wesley, John. The Use of Money. https://nbc.whdl.org/sites/default/files/resource/book/EN_John_Wesley_050 _use_ of_money.htm

Overcoming Addiction

Berridge, Kent C. and Morten L. Kringelbach. "Pleasure systems in the brain." Neuron 86, no. 3 (2015): 646–664.

Lembke, Anna. Dopamine Nation: Finding Balance in the Age of Indulgence. New York: Penguin Publishing Group, 2021.

Powledge, Tabitha M. Addiction and the brain: The dopamine pathway is helping researchers find their way through the addiction maze, BioScience, Volume 49, Issue 7, July 1999, Pages 513–519

Robinson, Terry E., and Bryan Kolb. "Structural plasticity associated with exposure to drugs of abuse." Neuropharmacology 47 (2004): 33-46.

Statistical References

Pastoral Care Inc. "Statistics in the Ministry." Pastoral Care Inc. Accessed November 19, 2023. www.pastoralcareinc.com/statistics.

Dr. Richard J Krejcir. PIR Ministries. Statistics on Pastors. https://pirministries.org/wp-content/uploads/2016/01/FASICLD-Statistics-on-Pastors.pdf

NAE. Majority of Pastors Suffer in Silence over Financial Challenges. www.nae.org/pastorresearch.

ABOUT THE AUTHOR

Dr. Susan Agbenoto, is an author, speaker, lay pastor as well as an investment performance professional. Her writings will navigate your perspectives into those beyond the physical, and will inspire you to boldly identify and grasp spiritual concepts you can practically apply. Susan obtained her Doctor of Ministry degree from The United Theological Seminary, during the COVID years, fulfilling a long-standing desire to delve more into theology.

Though she works with an Investment company and analyzes figures to articulate their embedded story, she still finds time to immerse herself in reading and fine-tuning various literary pieces and half-jokingly declares that "there is always more to write, but a book must have an end." Apart from writing, Dr. Agbenoto has been invited to speak in both religious and corporate forums. Outside of her writing adventures, Dr. Agbenoto likes to travel and experience the authenticity of other places, especially places with rich ecclesiastical narratives.

Her curiosity, faith, and love for God and his Word, immerses you into a place of restorative hope and renewal. Her conversational tone while explaining practical spiritual concepts make her books easy to read. Dr. Agbenoto's intertwining passions of prayer and the study of theology, translates into a tangible encounter with the divine as you read, leaving you intellectually stimulated, spiritually refreshed and wanting more. She is married, with two sons whom she adores.